YOU'RE HISTORY

EVERYDAY PEOPLE
EVERYDAY LIVES

PAUL TURNER

United Kingdom: Folens Publishers, Waterslade House, Thame Road, Haddenham, Buckinghamshire, HP17 8NT, UK
Email: folens@folens.com
Ireland: Folens Publishers, Greenhills Road, Tallaght, Dublin 24.
Email: info@folens.ie

Editor: Judi Hunter, Spellbound Books
Text design and layout: Redmoor Design, Tavistock, Devon
Picture researcher: Kayleigh Buller, Kate Greig, Sue Sharp
Illustrations: Ian Heard, Nick Hawken
Cover design: Jump To!
Harry Potter and the Philosopher's Stone – Copyright © J. K. Rowling 1997
Virgin Galactic

First published 2008 by Folens Limited.
Every effort has been made to contact copyright holders of material used in this publication. If any copyright holder has been overlooked, we should be pleased to make any necessary arrangements.
British Library Cataloguing in Publication Data. A catalogue record for this publication is available from the British Library.
ISBN   978-1-85008-352-8

You're History
Contents

Time is an interesting concept. It is only because we have clocks that we can see it passing by. Many people find it difficult to remember dates and to understand some of the terms used when discussing time. If this is a good description of you, perhaps this page will help.

Time Terms

Week: 7 days.

Month: 28 days during February (or 29 days in a leap year). 30 or 31 days in the remaining months.

Year: 365 days, or 366 days in a leap year.

Decade: 10 years.

Century: 100 years.

Millennium: 1000 years.

Centuries

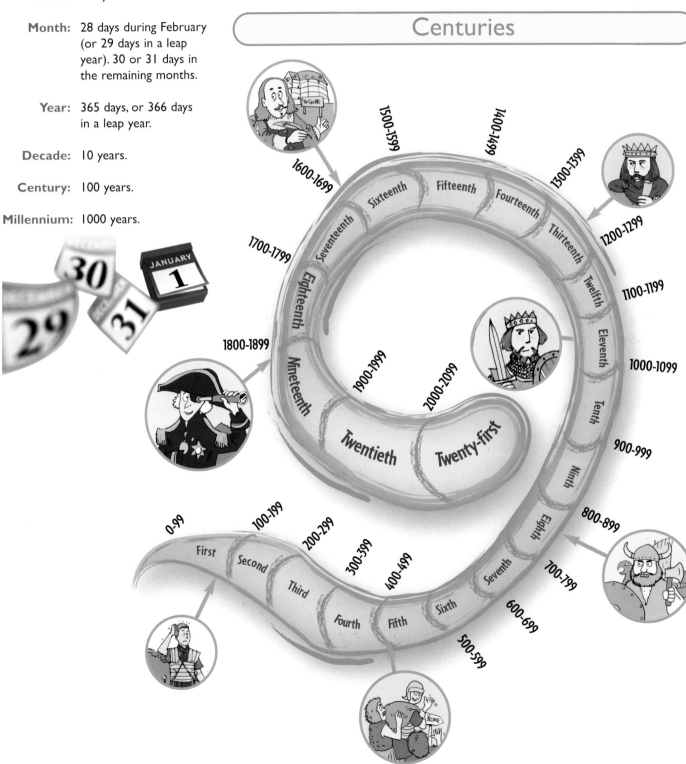

Introduction

Just when were the Middle Ages? Well, historians usually refer to the period between 1154 and 1485 as the Middle Ages. However, if we include the Norman Conquest, which was a significant turning point, the Middle Ages lasted from 1066 to 1485.

Who ruled ?

The Normans

1066–87	William the Conqueror (William I)
1087–1100	William II
1100–35	Henry I
1135–54	Stephen

The Plantagenets

1154–89	Henry II
1189–99	Richard I
1199–1216	John
1216–72	Henry III
1272–1307	Edward I
1307–27	Edward II
1327–77	Edward III
1377–99	Richard II

House of Lancaster

1399–1413	Henry IV
1413–22	Henry V
1422–61	Henry VI

House of York

1461–83	Edward IV
1483	Edward V
1483–85	Richard III

But this book isn't about kings and queens, it's about people like you!
So read on and find out about your ancestors…

This unit takes a look at what the country you know as Britain was like nearly 1,000 years ago.

Key questions you'll tackle will include:

- How do we know what life was like during the Middle Ages?
- What was the Domesday Book?
- What did people know about the world at this time?

Why Britain?

Millions of people live in Britain today and every year more people make it their home. Not only are the British Isles surrounded by seas rich in fish and animal life, they are crammed full of rivers, streams, fields, pastures, hedgerows and woodlands, all of which provide an abundance of natural food and materials. From a 21st century view-point, Britain also offers opportunities to set up businesses, make the most of good economic growth, and to live within a tolerant society.

Both **invaders** and **settlers** have made their way here for over 25,000 years. Look closely at our history and you'll find tales of Beaker people, Celts, Anglo Saxons, Romans, Jutes, Vikings and Normans. Because of the number of cultures that have influenced our own, the English language – sometimes called 'the language of the world' – is a mixture of words from numerous other languages. Much of it comes from Latin and French (**Latinate**), and German and Danish (**Germanic**). Modern British society, culture and language are all inspired and influenced by those who have made this island their home.

If we rewind time to the beginning of the Middle Ages, Britain as we know it today did not exist. England, Ireland, Scotland and Wales were all separate kingdoms, with few links. Massive changes eventually led to the formation of the United Kingdom, its **Empire** and **Commonwealth**. This book is about the lives of the people who lived on this island through that period of change. You'll learn about who they were, how they experienced life and what their thoughts and feelings were.

To do task 1

Warm up...

a) Name three other cultures that have influenced British culture as you understand it today.

b) Which king ordered the Domesday Book to be compiled?

c) Name two types of early world map.

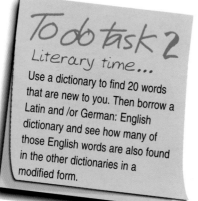

To do task 2

Literary time...

Use a dictionary to find 20 words that are new to you. Then borrow a Latin and /or German: English dictionary and see how many of those English words are also found in the other dictionaries in a modified form.

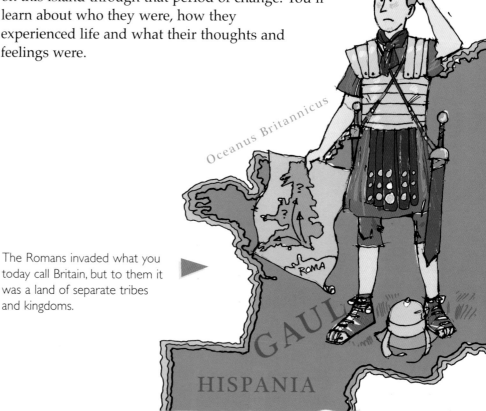

The Romans invaded what you today call Britain, but to them it was a land of separate tribes and kingdoms.

Oceanus Britannicus

ROMA

GAUL

HISPANIA

How do we know about so long ago?

The Norman Conquest of 1066 marks the start of a period of great change. It also marks the beginning of real record keeping, which helps us to know so much about what life was like then. The major source of evidence for what was going on in England during the Middle Ages, and for who lived there, is the **Domesday Book**, commissioned by William the Conqueror in 1085. 'Domesday' is the old English way of spelling Doomsday or Domesdei, a reference to Judgement Day.

Subjugate means to subdue or vanquish. It originates from a Latin word that literally meant 'bring under the yoke'.

Source A **England the Autobiography,** *John Lewis-Stempel (ed.),* Viking 2005

"So complete was William's inquisition of England that the subjugated English were put in mind of the day of judgement, hence the name for the register: 'The Domesdei (Doomsday) book'."

William had ordered that this 'Great Survey' be completed. It was similar to how a census would be carried out today. Although it was largely a way for William to see how much profit he could make from England, the Domesday Book also showed him exactly who lived in England in 1086 and how the population was made up. Actually two separate books, known as *Little Doomesday* and *Great Domesday*, it was written in Latin and shows us that during the Middle Ages there was a noticeable divide between rich and poor. Only 33% of the total population were classed as extremely poor and **impoverished**. The majority had a reasonable standard of life. Approximately 5% of the population owned most of the land and held the majority of the power. This is because, rather than living **democratically** like we do today, in the Middle Ages money and land meant power.

NB...

The Anglo Saxon Chronicle
Another record of the history of England and beyond was the Anglo-Saxon Chronicle. However this ceased to be compiled in the mid 12th century so tells us nothing after that time period.

Pages from the Domesday Book, now preserved in the National Archives in London.

Britain in the wider world

People in the Middle Ages did not know as much about the world around them as we do today. However, it might surprise you to learn that this didn't mean they had no idea at all. It just means that their knowledge was a bit sketchy and had some distinct flaws! Early maps of the world that survive today, such as the 'Mappa Mundi', show a number of these errors. Approximately 1,100 versions of the map survive around the world today, and if you're lucky enough to visit and see one, you may spot some differences. These maps represent the world as a flat circle rather than a globe, with Jerusalem and the Holy Land at the centre, and paradise and the figure of Jesus looming over it. Why they drew it like this no one knows because, contrary to popular belief, people did in fact know that the world was round.

Another surviving map called a Portolan Chart paints a slightly more accurate picture of the world, although still with errors. In general though, the medieval view of the world was better than many people realise, and over the Middle Ages people came to understand that Britain was just a small part of a much larger world.

The Hereford Mappa Mundi dates from around 1300. It is held in Hereford Cathedral.

Discussion POINT ?

Why is it important to have knowledge of the world around you?

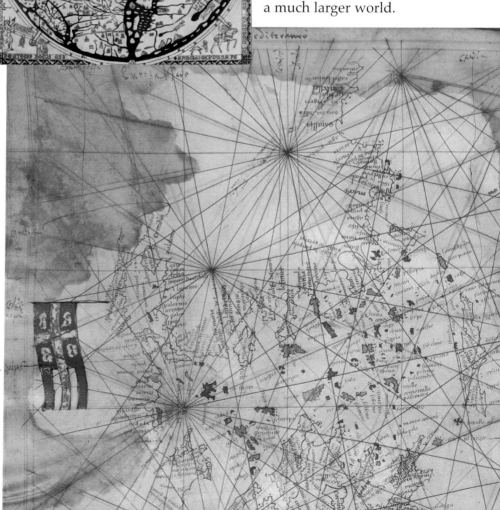

A Catalan Portolan Chart dating from 1325

Early maps were not easy to make and took a considerable amount of time and effort on the part of the map maker. It was more important to have a good knowledge of the seas than the land, and so map makers were less worried about how accurate countries were. Instead they tried to give as accurate a picture of the coasts and headlands as they could manage. They knew that this was what the sailors relied upon.

Modern technology today allows us to make very accurate and detailed maps. Satellite, computers and modern mapping equipment all accurately measure distances and so maps provide very accurate information about land and seas.

To do task 3
Get thinking...
In your own words, summarise why people have always liked to settle in Britain.

Source B — A beginner's guide to making a Portolan Chart

Portolan Charts were created by drawing a network of direction lines or 'rhumbs'. The chart maker drew a 'secret circle' around a central point, which he then bisected with straight lines. This gave 16 points on the circle's circumference, all of which were equidistant (at equal distances from each other). These points formed the location of another set of circles, which were then bisected in the same way.

The rhumb lines created by this method were used by the chart maker to plot the coastlines and by the sailors to plan their course. Different coloured inks were used to distinguish different directions.

To do task 4
Research it!
Conduct your own Domesday-style survey of your classmates.

Ask everybody who they live with, what animals they have, what style of house they live in, and any other questions that you think are appropriate. Land ownership in the Middle Ages was a key to power. What does your own survey tell you about the things that we value today?

To do task 5
Teamwork...
How much do you know about the world around you? Using a blank map of the world, work in teams to identify as many countries, continents and oceans as you can. Do you think you know more than someone living in the Middle Ages did?

Stop the clock
Remember that the Middle Ages began nearly 1000 years ago. To trace your family tree back that far would require you to research at least 30 generations!

We're starting to learn a bit about this time period, but what was every day life like?

For instance:

- How did people earn a living in the Middle Ages?
- What was a merchant?
- Who was the real Dick Whittington?
- Was life better in a town or a village?

Earning a living in a village

For people who lived in Medieval Britain, most lived their lives in a village so that is where they had to find employment. Being a largely **agricultural** country, most people had a farming job and these revolved around the cycle of the farming year. Jobs changed and often disappeared with the coming and going of the seasons. Planting and **harvesting** crops, tending to animals and ploughing fields made up the majority of the work, but over time other areas of work developed. These ranged from building houses and producing goods, to the manufacture of charcoal that could be used in the village.

Feudalism

Most people had to pay money or goods to the Lord of the Manor, usually 10% of their income. This was called a tithe and was part of a system called **feudalism,** which to most peasants was just the accepted way of life.

Above all, feudalism was a system of control. Based around the Lord of the Manor's estate, it forced people to work and sometimes fight for the privilege of staying on the land. However, some peasants resented being virtually owned by the local lord and wanted to make their own money. They began to do this through jobs such as fishing, mining and working in the increasing house-building trade.

King
The king owned all the land and kept about 20% of this land for his own use. The king granted the rest of this land to the Church and the barons

Church
About 25% of this land was granted to the Church. The Bishops (tenants-in-chief) granted land to their under-tenants. These men promised to supply knights when the king needed them.

Barons
About 55% of this land granted to the Barons. The Barons (tenants-in-chief) granted land to their under-tenants. These men promised to supply knights when the king needed them.

Under-Tenants
Under-tenants granted land to the peasants. In return, peasants provided rent or labour services

Under-Tenants
Under-tenants granted land to the peasants. In return, peasants provided rent or labour services.

Peasants
Serfs provided their labour in return for land. Free peasants paid a tithe instead of working for the Under-tenants.

 **Source A** An illustration of the feudal system

An illustration of the feudal system, Feudalism was based on the exchange of land for service, goods or money.

A country home

Houses often only had one room, shared by people and animals. Nobody had facilities we take for granted today, such as running water, heating or windows! A village property was simple, with walls made from **wattle and daub** and a thatched roof. Towards the end of the Middle Ages these houses began to improve. Houses with the luxury of a second level, a timber frame and strong stone foundations were making an appearance by the 13th century, and even the poorer classes could take advantage of these new building methods.

To do task 1

Think about...

People still have thatched roofs today. Find out what benefits this sort of roof has over slates or tiles.

Source B

The essence of wattle and daub constuction

Overlapping wattle strips – interwoven strips of wood – provided structure, and daub was laid on top. Typically daub was a mix of straw, mud and manure. Daub was actually mixed by hand – or foot – and spread on the wattle. When it dried it was virtually odourless.

The lure of the big city

Those people who did not want to live in a village had another option – the town. Medieval towns, although growing, were small in comparison to today, but were still busy places – home to a bustling collection of merchants and traders, and also to ordinary people who wanted to earn their fortunes or pick up work. By the 14th century approximately 600 towns provided a unique appeal, offering employment and a regular wage.

In the early 1300s around 20% of the population had migrated to towns to make the most of the employment and trading opportunities. Jobs existed within relatively large-scale manufacturing and trade and, on a smaller scale, in door-to-door selling. This move to towns reveals an important change in people's lives: seeking fortune in the town meant that you freed yourself from the feudal system, becoming a 'free' man. You were able to own money in your own right, and possibly even some land. For instance, anybody who entered the city of London to trade or find work was given a letter granting them permission to work. The 'freeman' then had to carry this letter around in a casket to show to anybody who wanted to see it.

Source C

This is a modern artist's idea of what a Medieval town looked like.

The world is getting smaller

As trade within and between towns was growing, a new role appeared – that of the **merchant**. Being a merchant was profitable as they were able to trade in new foreign goods transported to England by sea. Merchant ships with goods from home and abroad sailed into rivers and unloaded their goods for sale.

Throughout the Middle Ages, merchants were trading with nearby countries such as Flanders and France, and areas such as the Baltic. They imported – brought into the country – goods like wine and furs, and exported – sold out of the country – goods like leather and furniture.

These merchants were monitored by an organisation called the Merchant Guilds, which made sure that the merchants did everything by the book.

Guilds controlled trade in a town. They regulated prices, quality, weights and measures, and business practices. The power of the Guilds was very important because to be expelled from one made it impossible for a merchant to earn a living. Each Guild had a patron saint, celebrated religious festivals together, put on religious plays, and looked after the health and welfare of their members and their families.

Make me a masterpiece

People could also choose to become a craftsman rather than a merchant and they were regulated by an organisation called the Craftsman's Guild. To justify their status as a craftsman, employees had to work their way through a period of apprenticeship, which could take anywhere between two and seven years. Being an apprentice meant lots of hard work for very little reward. They got paid absolutely nothing, but on the plus side had their food, clothes and living costs paid for. They also had to stick to some very strict rules – see source E.

Source D

The merchant

The man pictured here is a 'mercer'. This type of merchant sold cloth, particularly silk or other fine fabrics. The clothes he wore were probably made from the same materials as he sold.

To do task 2

Research it!
People can still become a Master Craftsman today: what does it take to become one? Use the internet to research what the requirements are.

Source E

The Worst Children's Jobs in History

Tony Robinson,
Macmillan Children's Books, 2005

"Apprentices were not to hang around in pubs, not to gamble, not to get married or even engaged, to be sober, religious, polite and highly respectable."

Once their apprenticeship was completed, the apprentice earned the title of 'journeyman'. Journeyman comes from the French word 'journée', which means day, so the journeyman received his wages on a daily basis. This allowed the journeyman to work at their trade, eventually producing a 'masterpiece' of their own, which, if good enough, guaranteed them the title of 'craftsman'.

What a pantomime!

One of the most famous stories about seeking fame and fortune in a city is often performed as a pantomime. The tale of Dick Whittington may be familiar to you and is a real 'rags to riches' story of a poor boy making his way from Gloucester to London to seek out his fortune, with only his cat for company.

But did you know that, while it may be a Christmas pantomime show, it's based on a real person! Whittington was born in Gloucester sometime in the 1350s, and worked his way up through the cloth trade, helped in his journey by an apprenticeship to a gentleman called Sir Hugh Fitzwarren. Whittington eventually supplied cloth to both Richard II and Henry IV. He made so much money from his chosen career that he was even able to loan money to the king. His generosity also extended to the entire city of London, financing numerous projects such as the Guildhall library and the rebuilding of Newgate Gaol. Such was his popularity, Dick Whittington was made Mayor of London three times in total. History does not tell us whether he really owned a cat.

To do task 3

Get thinking…

Design an advert for an apprentice. Choose the trade you are offering the apprenticeship in, then include an illustration and as many facts as you can about what is involved.

BUZZ WORDZZ

Agricultural
Feudalism
Harvesting
Merchant
Wattle and daub

A contemporary illustration of Dick Whittington. Why do you think he is shown holding a skull?

Discussion POINT

From what you've read so far, which lifestyle would you choose – countryside or town?

13

The Ottoman Empire conquered Constantinople in 1453.

World Link

It's off to work we go!

A typical day's work in a town meant a lot of long, hard work. The day usually began at at 4 or 5am and only ended at 8 or 9pm. The start of the day was signalled by the ringing of the 'Angelus bell' and the day came to an end when the 'Curfew' bell was rung. Shops were open as early as 6am and the accompanying markets were noisy, busy places, full of shoppers and shouting merchants. Shops tended to be grouped together on streets whose names were linked to goods being sold on that street. Names like Bread Street, Fish Street and Cheese Street soon sprang up. Great examples of these Medieval streets still exist in towns around Britain today. The Shambles in York, for instance, is just such a street. Originally a row of butchers shops, the name came from the Saxon word 'fleshammels' literally meaning 'street of butchers'.

Stop the Clock

Westminster Abbey was built between 1045 and 1050. Remember this was the *11th* century.

To do task 4

Get creative...

a) Draw and label a storyboard about the true story of the life of Dick Whittington. Research the internet to find out extra facts. You could use Microsoft Paint to draw your pictures and then paste them into Microsoft Word.

b) Turn the storyboard into a pantomime performance of your own. Write a script, act it out and video it. You will really enjoy watching it!

To do task 5

Compare and contrast...

Find a modern advert for an apprentice. (You may need to look through a newspaper, telephone a company or look on the internet).
Compare the working conditions and expectations of an apprentice today to those of an apprentice in the Middle Ages. What differences can you identify? Why do you think this is?

Moving on from work, we come to someting equally important – food!

Most of us today don't have to think where our next meal is coming from but how was it for the average Medieval peasant?

- Were people hungry or did they eat well?
- Were table manners important?

Diet, mealtimes and choice

The population of the Middle Ages may not have had access to supermarkets and internet shopping, but they certainly didn't suffer from a lack of choice. Although there was not as much food available, variety was not an issue. Only in times of **famine** did the general population have difficulty feeding itself. Medieval citizens had no luxuries like fridges and freezers. Instead, they kept animals alive until they were needed, or salted the meat and fish in barrels. This could be quite expensive as they had to buy the salt, so an alternative was to hang the meat in the top of their house, smoking it over an open fire to preserve it.

People generally ate three times a day, although a fourth meal called 'nuntions' sometimes crept in. This was eaten at midday or 'noon'. People could do this because their meal times were different to ours. Breakfast was eaten very early, dinner usually around 10am and supper could be eaten as early as 3pm.

Bizarre but true: Porpoise was part of the Medieval diet.

Food glorious food

Villagers and people who lived in towns based their diet around oats, grains, bread and ale. Added to this was a wide variety of fruits and vegetables, most of which were grown in England. Their diet could be unusual, sometimes including hare, heron, swan, goose, squirrel, porpoise, hedgehog, carp, pike, trout, salmon, eel and herring. For dessert, you could enjoy fruit pies, peaches, redcurrants, blackcurrants, quince and many more fruits, often soaked in honey. This sort of food did not exist in large quantities, but if you lived in the towns you had a reasonable chance of being able to get them if you could afford them.

Drinking alcohol was also popular. So popular, in fact, that it was drunk every day. Products of farming are grain and hops and these are the essential ingredients of most ales. As towns grew, so did the problem of lack of clean water, so ale (and wine for the more wealthy) were suitable alternatives to this.

On special occasions large quantities of ale were required so people got brewing! Many of the young unmarried men of the village or town got

BUZZ WORDZZ

Customs
Famine
Alms

very excited about these occasions, mainly because they could down as much drink as they wanted for free, provided that they didn't fall down legless! If you lived close to a source of apples you could also enjoy cider to drink as an alternative to ale.

Watch your manners!

The rich observed many **customs** – they valued cleanliness and it was important to be seen to wash your hands before and after eating. Hands and faces were also wiped with napkins. This was balanced with something fun: they could eat their plates! These plates were called 'trenchers' and were made from bread cut into squares. This is where the term 'a square meal' comes from. You could eat the plate at the end of the meal or sometimes it was given to the very poor as a form of **alms**.

Meals could be long and consist of many courses but, no matter how enjoyable it was, licking your plate (provided that you hadn't already eaten it) was frowned upon.

Discussion POINT?

Which unusual Medieval foods would you like to try and why?

A wooden trencher, a basic plate that evolved from a square of stale bread

To do task 1

Get thinking...

Create a list of facts about eating in the Middle Ages. Choose the most interesting three facts in your opinion. Write a short paragraph to justify your decision.

To do task 2

Warm up...

a) How many times a day did people eat?

b) Name three types of food that were eaten during the Middle Ages that we do not eat today.

c) What was the name of the square plate made from bread?

To do task 3

Be creative...

Produce a menu for the Middle Ages, incorporating as many of the foods described on these pages as you can. Remember, people could not read, so your menu will need to be illustrated with appropriate pictures.

To do task 4

Research it!

Visit a modern supermarket. Take a list of food that the people ate in the Middle Ages. Compete against one of your friends to see who can find the most foods eaten in the Middle Ages. Compare your list to other people in the class. How many foods are eaten today that were also eaten in the Middle Ages?

Making your bowl

Most people in the Middle Ages prepared and ate their food using pottery bowls. Archaeologists use the discovery of this pottery as one of the main indications of settlement in an area. People usually made this pottery themselves using simple wheels or, more commonly, by spiralling coils of clay into the shape of a pot or bowl.

Healthy living

It may surprise you, but recent historical research shows that Medieval peasants may have had a healthier diet than much of 21st century Britain does! Today we eat a very high amount of sugar through cakes, biscuits and puddings, and especially through our breakfast cereal in the morning. We also do relatively little exercise, spending most of our day sitting down working, or in front of the television, computer or games console. Modern people therefore suffer from obesity, heart disease and other illnesses like high blood pressure and diabetes, all of which are a sign of the modern, lazy lifestyle many people lead.

Peasants had none of these problems, even though they had a shorter life expectancy. Their diet, which was high in unrefined grains and bread, and vegetables, meat, fish and ale was very healthy indeed. In fact many people today would benefit from following such a diet. Combined with the amount of hard work which they did – working on the land, ploughing fields, tending to animals, often for most of the hours of daylight available – they kept very healthy.

Today those who follow a similar diet, such as in places like Italy, are some of the healthiest people in Europe and live long, healthy lives now that diseases that previously killed people have been vaccinated against.

To do task 5

Get messy...

Have a go at creating your own 'trencher'. Use a large unsliced loaf of bread and ask an adult to help you cut out the shape. (You can do this with a normal knife that you would eat your tea with.) Once it is made, ask if you can eat your tea off it. Then eat your plate!

Let me entertain you!

People who lived in the Middle Ages didn't have the entertainment options that we have today. They had to rely on more basic entertainment, such as music. This was performed by travelling musicians called **troubadors,** who also acted as news reporters

Many instruments, often with unusual names, were popular – Hurdy Gurdy, Crumhorn, Rebec and the Shawn are all instruments that you may never even have heard of but they were big in Medieval Britain. The most famous musical instrument was the lute, which was very similar to a guitar.

With all that food and drink, people must have done something to get rid of all that energy!

This section will look at what that was:

- Did people have time to enjoy themselves in the Middle Ages?
- What did people do with their free time?
- What was jousting?

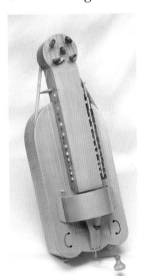  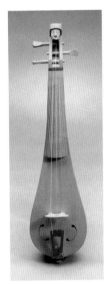

Medieval instuments: from left to right a Hurdy Gurdy, a Crumhorn and a Rebec.

The first game of football was in England in 1100.

The 'minstrel', which roughly translated means 'little servant', was a popular entertainer. There was very little that he couldn't do. He was the master of leaping, juggling, fire eating, magic and told a huge range of funny stories and songs.

Source A Medieval lives,
Terry Jones, BBC Books, 2004

"One 13th century poem defines a true minstrel as one who can 'speak and rhyme well, be witty, know the story of Troy, balance apples on the point of knives, juggle, jump through hoops, play the citole, mandora, harp, fiddle and psaltery'. He is further advised, for good measure, to learn the art of imitating birds, putting performing asses and dogs through their paces, and operating Marionettes."

BUZZ WORDZZ

Entertainment
Falconry
Jousting
Nobility
Swordsmanship
Troubadors

Discussion POINT ?

Should we celebrate our holy days and saint days more enthusiastically?

I need a break!

People in the Middle Ages had an estimated eight weeks' holiday per year to enjoy whatever **entertainment** there was to be had. Most people also had Sundays off to rest and relax, and numerous annual holidays meant another day off for many people. On festival days such as St Valentine's Day, May Day and over the Easter period, people got involved in sporting contests, like archery, hammer throwing, stool ball and wrestling. They might also have had a go at card games and board games like 'Nine Men's Morris' and 'Knucklebones'.

Fancy a joust?

Jousting – a sport often associated with the Middle Ages – was popular. Two riders on horseback rode at each other, either side of a four-foot high wooden barrier. Each carried a long jousting lance with which he tried to hit his opponent, and knock him off his horse. The lance, which was very weak and snapped easily, was carried in the right hand. It could be up to 4m long, and often had a blunted end rather than a sharp point so as not to impale the opponent by accident. 'Riding at the ring' was another popular variation on jousting – the aim being to get the lance through a ring that had been suspended in the air. Competing in these sports was reserved for the **nobility**, but anybody could watch.

The contest was taken very seriously. Often specific challenges would be issued. Huge crowds attended, attracted through colourful pamphlets and displays of banners and posters. Knights fought for the love of a woman, who would give them a token of their affection if they won. They also had the added incentive of prize money.

Jousting was not the only sport that took place on these contest days.

Displays of **swordsmanship** also took place, along with displays of **falconry**.

The ancient skill of training birds of prey is still going strong in Britain today. Falconry displays are a popular part of the summer tourist calendar at castles or stately homes.

To do task 1

Warm up...

a) Name three types of instrument that were played in the Middle Ages.

b) How many weeks holiday a year did people have during this period?

c) What is jousting?

To do task 2

Be creative...

Imagine that you are designing the itinerary for a modern re-enactment of a Medieval festival. Outline all the activities that you would include. How would you attract people to come along? What explanations might you need to add for a modern audience?

To do task 3

Get active...

Research the rules for 'Nine Men's Morris' and 'Knucklebones'. Hold a class competition of either game and see if you can win!

For many people today, religion is not a big part of their life. However you need to understand that in the Middle Ages, it was very different:

- How religious were people in the Middle Ages?
- Why did some people devote their whole lives to religion?
- Who – or what – what was an alchemist?

Source A

A Little History of the English Country Church,
Roy Strong,
Jonathan Cape, 2007

"The Church taught that the souls in Purgatory could be helped both by the prayers of the living and by the offering of the Eucharist on their behalf. In Hell the deceased found themselves in a torture chamber where the smallest pain they endured exceeded the greatest pain on Earth. Punishment fitted the crime; the gluttonous were fed on toads and serpents; the proud were bound to wheels covered by burning hooks."

Regular worship

Religion and a belief in the afterlife were powerful, important parts of people's lives during the Middle Ages. The dominant religion in Britain during this time was Roman Catholicism. The local village priest usually lived within the community and accepted a life-long following of religion and its values.

Most churches were small and were built by the local lord and controlled by the diocese, with a bishop being placed in charge. They were distributed randomly across the country with no set pattern. People attended church regularly. They were very afraid of what was known as **purgatory**.

Purgatory was the place of judgement, suspended between heaven and earth, where a decision was made about your future. Those sent to purgatory would be punished before finally being allowed through the 'Pearly gates' into heaven.

What picture of Hell did the church paint and why do you think they did this?

Going on a pilgrimage

Many people made a religious **pilgrimage** during their lifetime. The visit would usually be for a specific reason – to pay a visit to the shrine of a saint, or to seek a miracle like the healing of an illness or disease. However the pilgrim might ask for help on their journey through purgatory into heaven. Popular pilgrimage destinations in Britain were Westminster Abbey (to visit Edward the Confessor's shrine) and Canterbury (to visit Thomas Becket's shrine). Edward the Confessor died in 1066 and he is the Roman Catholic patron saint of kings. Thomas Becket had been the Archbishop of Canterbury between 1118 and 1170, but he was brutally murdered by four knights who believed they were acting on the wishes of their king, Henry II.

A quiet life?

Some people chose to devote their whole life to the service of God. They were known as monks and nuns and they lived a very religious lifestyle. People still make this lifestyle choice today. The job of a monk or a nun during the Middle Ages was meant to be very simplistic. It generally involved praying, gardening, tending to the sick, and because monks were some of the few people who could read and write at the time, a good deal of their time was spent copying beautifully crafted manuscripts.

Who wants to be a millionaire?

You might not think this fits with their holy lifestyle but, in reality, the monasteries and convents had a lot of money and many monks and nuns didn't live as quiet and religious a lifestyle as history might lead like you to believe.

See sources B and C for details...

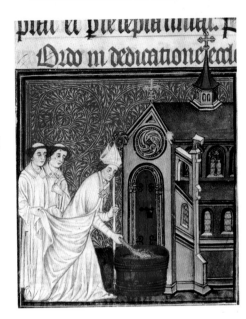

Part of a 14th-century illuminated manuscript, showing the consecration of a church by a bishop with monks helping him.

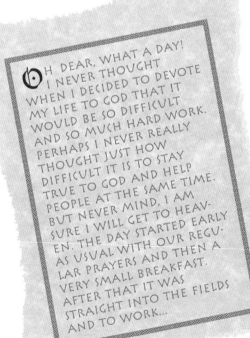

OH DEAR, WHAT A DAY! I NEVER THOUGHT WHEN I DECIDED TO DEVOTE MY LIFE TO GOD THAT IT WOULD BE SO DIFFICULT AND SO MUCH HARD WORK. PERHAPS I NEVER REALLY THOUGHT JUST HOW DIFFICULT IT IS TO STAY TRUE TO GOD AND HELP PEOPLE AT THE SAME TIME. BUT NEVER MIND, I AM SURE I WILL GET TO HEAVEN. THE DAY STARTED EARLY AS USUAL WITH OUR REGULAR PRAYERS AND THEN A VERY SMALL BREAKFAST. AFTER THAT IT WAS STRAIGHT INTO THE FIELDS AND TO WORK...

To do task 1

Get creative...

The churches in the Middle Ages often exhibited 'doom' paintings that showed images of heaven, purgatory and hell. One of these is shown on this page. Create your own doom painting showing what **you** think heaven, purgatory and hell would be like.

Alchemists
Artefacts
Indulgences
Pilgrimage
Purgatory

To do task 2
Sources...

a) What do sources B and C suggest that monks' and nuns' lives were really like?

b) How reliable and useful are these sources to someone studying the lives of Medieval monks and nuns?

Source B

History Without the Boring Bits,

Ian Crofton, Quercus, 2007

"The Nuns of St Helen Bishopsgate in the City of London were reprimanded for kissing members of the public and wearing over-ostentatious veils; at the same time the prioress was ticked off for keeping too many lapdogs. This rebuke seems to have had little effect, for in 1439, the Nuns were told to desist from 'dancing and revelling', except at Christmas, and then only among themselves."

Source C

Medieval Lives, *Terry Jones, BBC Books, 2004*

"No well-to-do monk wanted to sleep in a cold dormitory with all the other monks, so since the infirmary was the only place where a fire was allowed, monks with money began to move in there, establishing individual 'bachelor pads' – each with a private room with its own fireplace and with a bedroom above, complete with en-suite lavatory."

Many monks and nuns made their money through the sale of relics or religious **artefacts**. **Indulgences** (holy relics), designed to buy you forgiveness or a speedy entry to heaven, were sold for a tidy profit.

Move over Harry Potter!

In the Middle Ages, if people didn't want to rely entirely on God to provide them with eternal life, there were other options open to them. A strange way of seeking enlightenment, and possibly eternal life, was through the art of 'alchemy'.

Alchemists themselves were men who – bizarrely – were sometimes described as having an odour about them similar to a goat! They generally shrouded themselves in secrecy and cut themselves off from society.

Discussion POINT

Would it be good to find something that guaranteed you eternal life?

A modern impression of how an alchemist might have worked. Does this match the sort of image you have in your mind when you think about wizards?

NB...

We may not have alchemists any more but people still search for eternal youth. What makes some people want to have cosmetic surgery, or constantly try and avoid the ageing process?

The central belief in alchemy was that elements could be changed by rearranging the four qualities that made up the metals most people were familiar with: dryness, coldness, moisture and heat. The physical part of the process was the attempt to turn a base metal – lead – into a precious metal – gold. The spiritual part was to purify oneself through a strange, mystical process, often involving secret symbols and pictures.

Very little is really known about what we'd now describe as chemistry. Not only were the alchemists pursuing an easy path to riches, they were also hunting for an elixir of life to keep them on this earth for longer than usual. The art is shrouded in mystery and secrecy and the people who practised it used dreams and visions to help them achieve their goals. It was hardly scientific. Sometimes the alchemists struck gold, so to speak, but this was not real. It was actually called 'butter of gold', made by mixing gold dust with mercury and powdered silver.

Alchemists and their mysterious actions still captivate audiences today. One very famous alchemist called Nicholas Flamel was even mentioned in the Harry Potter books…

To do task 3

Warm up…

a) What was the main religion in Britain in the Middle Ages?

b) Give two ways in which monks and nuns made money.

c) What was alchemy?

To do task 4

Get thinking…

If you could interview an alchemist, what five questions would you ask him? Write these down and compare them to a friend's.

Stop the clock

In 1188, Newgate prison was built in London.

Source D

The Alchemist
Harry Potter and the Philospher's Stone,
J K Rowling, Bloomsbury 1997

"Nicholas Flamel", she whispered dramatically, "is the only known maker of the Philosopher's Stone!"

This didn't have quite the effect she'd expected. "The what?" said Harry and Ron.

"Oh, honestly, don't you two read? Look – read that, there."

She pushed the book towards them, and Harry and Ron read:

"The ancient study of alchemy is concerned with making the Philosopher's Stone, a legendary substance with astonishing powers. The Stone will transform any metal into pure gold. It also produces the Elixir of Life, which will make the drinker immortal.

There have been many reports of the Philospher's Stone over the centuries, but the only Stone currently in existence belongs to Mr Nicholas Flamel, the noted alchemist and opera lover. Mr Flamel, who celebrated his six hundred and sixty-fifth birthday last year, enjoys a quiet life in Devon with his wife, Perenelle (six hundred and fifty eight.)"

I'm not feeling too well!

In the Middle Ages people didn't have much chance of a long life. In general, people could expect to live for around 30 years. A lot less was known about germs and disease and only basic health care was available. Children often died very young, sometimes very soon after birth, and childbirth itself was a very risky procedure for women too. Not even the use of **Caesarean sections** – a technique known about since Roman times – did much to improve the situation.

Bigger towns and cities offered people the chance to attend hospitals. In London, for example, St Mary's, St Bartholomew's and St Thomas' welcomed patients, although the standard of care available in them was nowhere near what we expect today

In Britain today you're fortunate to have GPs and hospitals provided to keep you fit and healthy. In the Middle Ages things were quite different. Here we'll consider:

- How healthy were people in the Middle Ages?
- Was it easy to get a good doctor?
- What was the Black Death and how was it caught?

Leeches and other cures

Cures for illnesses had very little grounding in science or common sense. Some appear as little more than madness, but people did not have the scientific understanding that we possess today so they were not stupid, just desperate to try anything for a cure.

One method that has survived the test of time is small, black and lives in ponds – the leech. Leeches were used when a doctor believed that the patient needed 'bleeding'. A leech could be applied to any area of the body – even the more personal, sensitive areas – to draw out quantities of blood. Blood letting is also known as **phlebotomy**, which is a term now associated with taking blood samples. Leeches are still used in medicine today.

A leech being used on a patient in a hospital in the USA. Their use is to remove blood with little oxygen in it, which helps reduce swelling and encourages fresh blood to flow and heal the area.

Perhaps you would like to try some other Medieval cures? If you are feeling ill, wear red. A warm colour will warm you up. If you have a fever, drink water **infused** with a boiled horse's hoof. If there's anybody in your family who is mad, find a porpoise, skin it and whip the patient with the skin. If somebody needs sedating, give them stewed brain of squirrel in wine.

Source A

A Tudor Medicine Chest,
Brian Moses,
Hodder Wayland, 2002

"The heads of mice being burned and beaten into powder is excellent for the scouring and cleansing of the teeth. This powder is called Toothsoap."

Source B The Curious Cures of Old England,
Nigel Cawthorne,
Portrait Books, 2005

"By Medieval times things had moved on and most internal illnesses were thought to be caused by bosom serpents – snakes, worms, frogs, toads and lizards that took up residence in the parts of the body affected. Patients would regularly vomit up reptiles. The cure was a draft of horse's urine, which was guaranteed to flush them out. Or you could dangle a piece of bread on a hook and lower it down the patient's throat."

Fancy a hair cut?

With no GP to visit, people visited a **barber surgeon** instead. Medieval barber surgeons were not really specialists in anything other than cutting hair, yet they tried a lot of other things. They acted as amateur dentists, surgeons and GPs all in one. Imagine going to get your hair cut and having a tooth pulled out, or an operation at the same time!

To do task 1

Sources...

What ingredient in toothpaste may have actually worked and cleaned the teeth?

Source C

A Tudor Medicine Chest,
Brian Moses,
Hodder Wayland, 2002

"When a young girl enters the surgery complaining of 'shivery ague' the surgeon lifts a jar of live spiders from the medicine chest. Dipping one in butter, he places it, still wriggling, on the poor girl's tongue. Holding her nose, she gulps it down. The wriggling of the spider, says the surgeon, will cure the shivering of the ague."

A barber surgeon would test urine samples by holding the flask up to the light and then checking its colour, smell and taste. Examining the top of the sample showed problems with the head and brain, the middle represented the heart, lungs and stomach and the bottom of the sample represented the body from the waist down.

Feeling ill?
One disease that is widely associated with the Middle Ages is the Black Death. A devastating plague, the Black Death struck Britain in 1348, 1361, 1368, 1376 and 1390, amongst other years, although the greatest devastation occurred in the last six months of 1348 when over 1.5 million people died.

Traditionally historians believed the Black Death arrived in Britain from overseas via a port, and there is no reason to doubt that theory. The most viable entry points for the disease to Britain are the ports of Melcombe (now Weymouth), Southampton and Bristol. The disease crept its way up the country, starting in the South West.

What was the Black Death?

The Black Death is almost unidentifiable as a pure disease. It is a mixture of other diseases – **bubonic, septicaemic** and **pneumonic** plague. The disease is not naturally present amongst a human population. It is transmitted to people through fleas that live on rodents but could be passed on by squirrels and mice as well as rats. The bacteria live successfully within the bloodstream of rats and when the flea bites the animal, it takes on the bacteria, which are then able to multiply within its body. The flea, once infected, moves on to another animal (and in Medeival times this could easily have been a human), and passes on the disease.

The Black Death, despite being a mixture of three different types of plague, traditionally shows symptoms of bubonic plague. Victims suffered from pus-filled boils developing all over their body. These boils – or buboes – were a particularly unpleasant growth that could be as big as an orange. This was not the only symptom of the disease – others included vomiting, diarrhoea, fever and bleeding under the skin.

Characteristics of the other plague types include:

Pneumonic plague. This disease almost appears to be worse than the bubonic plague – attacking a person's lungs and leading to the victim coughing up alarming amounts of blood.

Septicaemic plague. This is a blood disease, which multiplies inside the body and kills without any warning. It too can be passed on by fleas. The effects of septicaemic plague can be so bad that victims are made hysterical by seeing blood streaming out of their nose and mouth.

The plague spanned all gaps within society. It attacked both rich and poor without prejudice. It earned the name 'the great mortality' because so many people died. The problem was made worse by poor living conditions and lack of hygiene. Bubonic plague still kills around 2000 people each year today, but it is by no means as dangerous in the modern world as other diseases.

Stop the Clock

The Black Death reached Scotland in 1350.

Source D

Ian Crofton, *History Without the Boring Bits,* Quercus, 2007

"The Tartars besieging Kaffa (modern Theodosia in the Crimea, then governed by the Genoese) catapulted the corpses of their own men who had died of plague into the city, in the hope that this would spread the disease to the defenders. It is thought that the Black Death may have spread to Europe via Genoese traders fleeing the city."

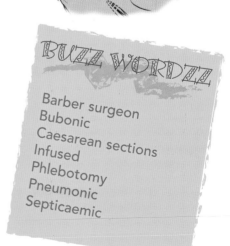

BUZZ WORDZZ

Barber surgeon
Bubonic
Caesarean sections
Infused
Phlebotomy
Pneumonic
Septicaemic

Source E

Medicine,
Paul Strathern,
Robinson, 2005

"The French physician Guy de Chauliac said that the only cure for plague was 'fugo cito, vade longe, rede tarde', which means 'flee speedily, go far away, and return slowly'."

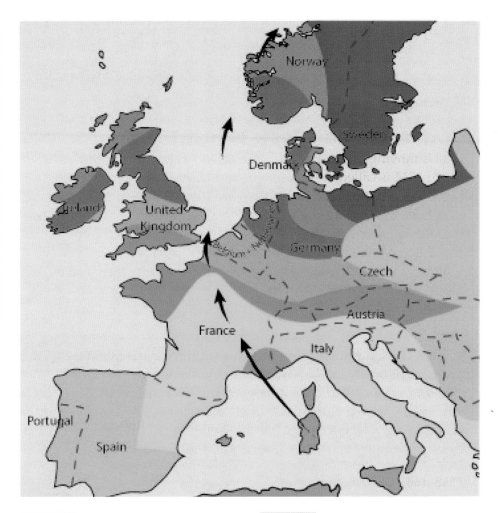

▪ December 1347		▪ December 1349	
▪ June 1348		▪ June 1350	
▪ December 1348		▪ December 1350	
▪ June 1349		– – – Country Borders	

Map showing the spread of the Black Death across 14th-century Europe. ▲

To do task 2
Get messy...

Create your own plague make-up, giving a friend a buboe and some bruising to make it look as if they have the Black Death. Once they are made-up, take their photograph and get the whole class to take photos showing different stages of the plague. Use 'Movie-Maker' to add video, voiceover, music and sound effects if you wish.

To do task 3
Warm up...

a) What was the average life expectancy of people who lived in the Middle Ages?

b) Describe two cures for illness from this period.

c) When did the Black Death strike in England?

To do task 4
Get thinking...

Design a PowerPoint presentation about the Black Death. Explain how it spread, the various symptoms and possible cures. You are only allowed to use four slides, so choose the four most important pieces of information.

Discussion POINT ?

Could you have coped with the horrible cures of the Middle Ages?

Chapter 2

What was everyday life like for people in Tudor and Stuart Britain?

Introduction

Time is moving on, and now we'll start looking at what came after the Middle Ages. The period from 1485 to 1714 is called Tudor and Stuart Britain, named after the royal houses whose kings ruled Britain between those dates. In fact, this chapter also makes some references to events and changes that occurred up to 1750. In this way, it also covers the Protectorate (when England did not have a king), the reign of the House of Orange and part of the House of Hanover.

Who ruled ?

House of Stuart

| 1603–25 | James I |
| 1625–49 | Charles I |

House of Tudor

1485–1509	Henry VII
1509–47	Henry VIII
1547–53	Edward VI
1553	Lady Jane Grey
1553–58	Mary I
1558–1603	Elizabeth I

Commonwealth and Protectorate

1649–53	Council of State
1653–58	Oliver Cromwell
1658–59	Richard Cromwell

House of Stuart (restored)

1660–85	Charles II
1685–88	James II
1689–94	William III and Mary II (joint)

Orange & Stuart

| 1694–1702 | William III |
| 1702–14 | Anne |

House of Hanover

| 1714–27 | George I |
| 1727–60 | George II |

But as we said at the start, this book isn't about kings and queens.
It's about ordinary people like you!

We've moved on from the Middle Ages, and need to find out if houses and living conditions had changed at all. Think about:

- Were Tudor and Stuart houses any better than those of the Middle Ages?

- What was a typical house like at this time?

- What impact did the Great Fire of London have on housing and living conditions in London and nationwide?

BUZZ WORDZZ

Pamphlets
Prefabricated

This Tudor building at Elstow in Bedfordshire is a preserved example of a moot hall, and would have been used as a meeting point for deciding local area issues.

What a lovely house!

The main links that we have with the Tudor and Stuart periods are the magnificent houses that are still standing. A far cry from the early wattle and daub houses that many villagers lived in, they were a natural evolution from the castles of the Middle Ages. The big houses were built by merchants and successful businessmen of the day, and their lifestyles matched the houses that they lived in. They sat on elaborate furniture, slept in oak beds and wrapped themselves in rich materials. Their four poster beds still conjure up a romantic picture. Plastered or wood-panelled walls were all the rage. Tapestries depicting stories from the Bible and traditional stories from history covered the walls.

Building materials were not scarce. A lot of the stone that was used to build these houses had come from the monasteries that had been stripped and destroyed, on the orders of King Henry VIII in the mid 16th-century.

Build me a home!

New houses needed house builders and this was an opportunity for many people to become involved in the house building industry on a larger scale. Labourers were needed to make the bricks, lay the foundations, source the materials and build the houses. The master builder was another skilled profession that could be entered into after an apprenticeship, and the stone mason also had an important role to play. Both jobs had attractive prospects and a lot of potential.

Home sweet home!

The poorer population lived more modest lives, in simpler houses, with simpler possessions. In place of the fancy furniture, people had simple chairs, tables and beds. Sometimes there was so little room that the entire family had to sleep in one bed. These poorer houses were decorated with posters and **pamphlets** pasted to the walls.

The growth of the towns had meant that new styles of houses were becoming popular and they now had as many as three or four stories. The temptation was for the houses to be built poorly, with little regard for the people living in them, but some were well built. A novel way to move house was to do just that – move it. Wooden-framed houses were put up quickly and could also be taken down quickly and moved to another place. **Prefabricated** houses could also be put up in record time, some of which had quality brick chimneys and glazed windows.

These houses were by no means plain, with beautifully-coloured, silvery oak beams and coloured plaster, sometimes blue or pink. Some daring people went even as far as using hand-printed wallpaper to decorate their walls.

To do task 1
Get thinking...
Houses in this period were very diffferent to those today. If you were asked to describe the housing what would you say? What key features would you focus on ?

Discussion POINT ?
Would you have put up with poor living conditions in order to find work?

Or not so sweet...

As towns grew in popularity some people had to put up with over-crowded living conditions or hastily-built houses. Disease spread even more quickly. Local laws were eventually introduced to guarantee the quality of the houses, but quite often this was not effective. Fire was also a very real hazard amongst the crowded, cramped streets. And just such a fire took place in the 17th century, becoming one of the greatest events in British history! Read on...

London's burning!

The Great Fire of London started on Sunday 2 September 1666, caused by a spark from a fire in a bakery on Pudding Lane. It quickly spread, the flames made considerably worse by a strong wind blowing from the east. With no professional fire service existing, Londoners attempted to put the fire out themselves, using mainly leather fire buckets full of water. There were some primitive fire engines but they arrived too late to help, or were too clumsy to use to be effective.

Their attempts did not have the desired effect and by the time Monday morning came approximately 300 houses had been burnt to the ground. Others had been sacrificed and pulled down in an attempt to stop the fire spreading further. People left London as they feared for their lives and the city was only saved when the decision was made to blow up houses in the path of the fire with gunpowder. This created a firebreak – an area where there was nothing for the flames to consume, so allowing it to die down. The fire was out completely by Thursday 6th September but had destroyed nearly 13,000 houses and 87 churches. The city had been devastated.

The devastation meant that the houses and important buildings had to be rebuilt. Major architectural redesign of buildings such as St Paul's Cathedral was entrusted to people like Sir Christopher Wren and some of these buildings have survived into the modern era. However, the opportunity to completely demolish all the poor quality housing was lost, mainly due to the rights of the house owners. They were given the choice to rebuild their homes on the same plot of land, and many wanted to do that.

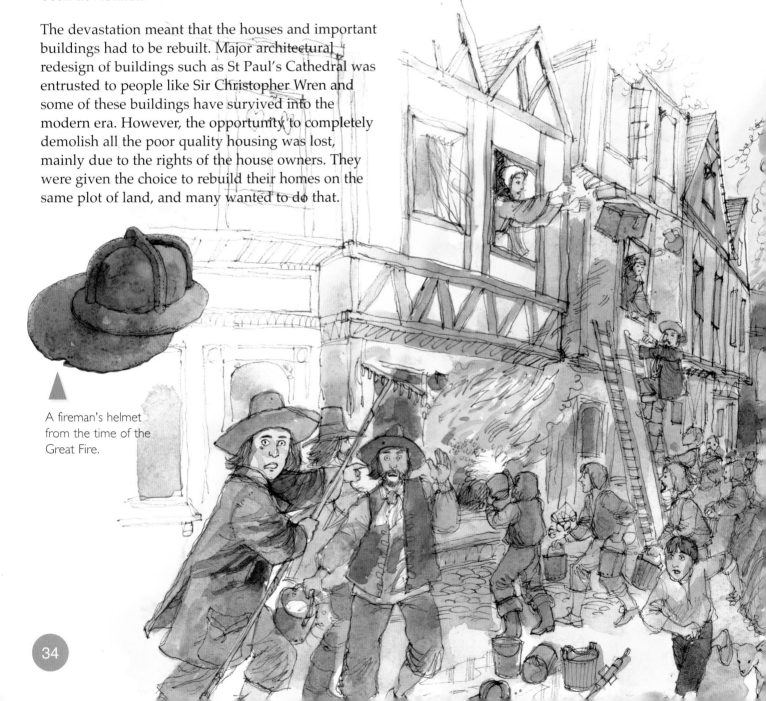

A fireman's helmet from the time of the Great Fire.

After the fire

In the aftermath of the Great Fire insurance companies were established by entrepreneurs like Nicholas Barbon, who set up the London Fire Company. Large insurance companies like Lloyds of London were also formed. However, they only insured houses made from brick. To prevent losses from another incident like the Great Fire, these insurance companies also set up the early fire brigades to safeguard future losses.

A fire insurance plaque, which would have been attached to a building showing the owner had insurance against fire, and therefore the fire brigade would tackle the fire.

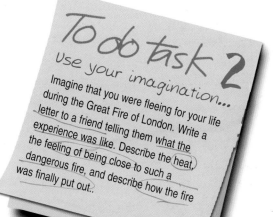

To do task 2

Use your imagination...

Imagine that you were fleeing for your life during the Great Fire of London. Write a letter to a friend telling them what the experience was like. Describe the heat, the feeling of being close to such a dangerous fire, and describe how the fire was finally put out..

To do task 3

Get active...

a) In groups of four (or pairs if your class is small), write a news broadcast about the events of the Great Fire of London. If your teacher has an interactive whiteboard, they can project a background image on to the screen.

b) Video your news broadcast and play it back to the rest of the class. Remember, it must be factually correct. People are relying on you to give them the truth!

To do task 4

Back to the future...

Compare the housing and living conditions in the Tudor and Stuart periods to the conditions today. How do they differ, and are there any similarities?

Providing care for the poor in society is not a modern issue: Here we'll look at what ideas were around in the Tudor and Stuart period, and you'll understand:

- What was a vagabond?
- How were the poor looked after?

I'm so poor!

The amount of **poverty** in Tudor and Stuart Britain was startling, and it highlights a huge gap in quality of life that existed during this period. A number of factors and circumstances led to there being many unemployed and poor people. The dissolution of the monasteries and a high number of unemployed soldiers and sailors were two of the largest factors. The growing population meant that generally jobs were harder to come by, and this alone would have meant that some people faced hardship. However, in a relatively small period of time, this was made worse by failed harvests, a fall in wages and a change in farming methods. Labour-**intensive** crop farming evolved into sheep farming, which required relatively few people.

Old farming methods changed and as a result, there were fewer jobs in agriculture.

Who were the poor?

More people were forced to wander the streets looking for work. **Vagrants** and **vagabonds** were one of the biggest problem groups for the king – and later the government – at this time. The unemployed and homeless began to move around the country, looking for work They even resorted on occasion to riot and protest. People were genuinely afraid of these menacing mobs. Something had to be done. The king and later Parliament tried many ways to control this wandering group, including punishment and charity. Many people believed that they were responsible for a rise in crime – usually assaults and thefts.

Can we control the poor?

In 1601 a law was introduced that aimed to solve this problem. A poor rate was to be raised that would **supplement** the income of these people, payable by the rich. As you can imagine they were not very happy about it! By 1700 the amount collected had risen to around £700,000. Yet even this did not solve the problem of the poor, and the vagabonds – also known as "the idle poor"– continued to create unrest with their money-making schemes and **deceptions**. If caught begging, their punishment ranged from whipping, to being branded on the chest or face with a letter 'V', or having a hole bored through their ear. Parishes also built places to house the wandering poor, with the first **workhouses** set up in 1550.

BUZZ WORDZZ

Deceptions
Intensive
Poverty
Supplement
Vagabonds
Vagrants
Workhouses

Vagabonds

The vagabonds were a particular problem in this period as they wandered from place to place, claiming benefits in the form of money or shelter. Often benefits could be claimed from numerous areas without anybody knowing that the vagabond had already claimed from another area. Vagabonds were rarely brought to justice because of the lack of an effective police force as we know it today. The village constable, a volunteer, was often told old, or too busy, to catch the criminals. On those rare occasions when they were caught, vagabonds were punished harshly. They could be whipped, placed in the stocks, branded on the face, or mutilated. The stocks were an early form of punishment that publicly humiliated the criminal. He or she would sit down on the ground and place their legs through two holes cut into two pieces of wood, which were then locked shut over the legs. The vagabond would then be left and forced to sit – often in the town square – for a day or sometimes longer. Mutilation involved nose slitting or cutting off parts of the ear to indicate that the person was a vagabond.

An important distinction must be made between vagabonds and vagrants. Vagabonds were "idle" and had no intention of working – except working hard at deceiving people! Vagrants were the genuinely poor who needed help surviving either because they had lost their job, or had fallen ill and could not work.

Vagabonds were a strange mix of people, both male and female, who relied on tricks or sympathy for "fake" wounds or ailments. They had names like "Bawdy Basket", "Ruffler", "Abraham man" and "Doxy" to name but a few.

Discussion POINT

How would you solve the problem of the Tudor poor?

Stop the clock

In 1681, the first oil lighting was seen in England.

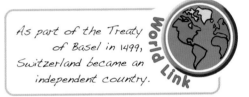

As part of the Treaty of Basel in 1499, Switzerland became an independent country.

World Link

A contemporary French illustration showing vagabonds and how to spot them.

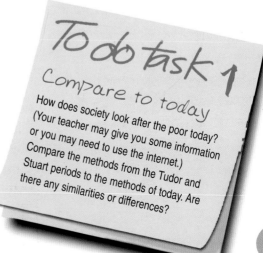

To do task 1

Compare to today

How does society look after the poor today? (Your teacher may give you some information or you may need to use the internet.) Compare the methods from the Tudor and Stuart periods to the methods of today. Are there any similarities or differences?

37

As we look at the past we've come accross early ideas about medicine and health, but now we'll consider if medical knowledge had improved since the Middle Ages.

For example:

- How were diseases and illnesses cured?
- Was the Great Plague similar to the Black Death, and what impact did it have in Britain?

A woodcut showing a barber surgeon at work extracting teeth.

Doctor, doctor!

Some advances had been made in medicine between the Middle Ages and this period, but not many. Disease and illness killed far more people than they do today and life expectancy was still very low. A long life for some people during this period meant not much more than 30 years. In fact, many men didn't see far past 20 years. Women could expect to live longer, but would be classed as 'old' when they reached 40. The richer classes would enjoy longer lives, although you had done well if you got past 50 years old.

Childbirth was still very dangerous, even with more regular use of Caesarean sections, and the number of children who died in the first few years of life was still at a high level.

Doctors were now licensed, although they were by no means experts. They were granted a licence based on their perceived ability to do their job. This meant that a doctor could be distinguished from a barber surgeon, which might guarantee a better standard of treatment. **Dissection** of bodies began to occur during this period, which further increased the knowledge of the human body. The following extract is from an early **autopsy** by William Harvey.

Source A) **England the Autobiography,** *John Lewis-Stempel (ed.),* Penguin Books, 2005

"The heart was large, thick and fibrous with a considerable mass of fat around its walls and partition. The blood in the heart was blackish, liquid and scarcely grumous. Only in the right ventricle were some clots seen."

William Harvey

William Harvey was the pioneer of much modern medical knowledge. Born in 1578 in Folkestone, his father was a rich businessman. Harvey studied at both Caius College Cambridge and the University of Padua and spent a long time working at St Bartholomew's Hospital before he was made the physician of both James I and Charles I. Surprisingly perhaps, his successes came when he was in his 50s, and his ideas on **circulation** of the blood were shared and discussed. They would eventually change the whole approach to medicine and health.

They don't know what they're talking about – try this!

Although pioneers like Harvey were beginning to make breakthroughs, the old cures were still thought to be the best. Blood was often removed from the body in such quantities that nearly three litres could be drained away, which is about half the amount in your body. An odd technique, **scarification**, was used to increase the number of cuts that could be made quickly and, therefore, increase the amount of blood that could be taken.

This is because people still didn't fully understand what caused disease. Cures centred around avoiding stagnation of the blood, which was believed to happen as blood was used up. Stagnated blood was bad, so the best solution was to remove it from the body. Also there was wide acceptance that the four humours of the body needed to be in balance. These ideas dated back to Ancient Greek knowledge, and blood was the dominant humour and so it needed balancing most. Again, the solution was to remove blood from the body – often in quantity!

A portrait of William Harvey (1578 – 1657).
Harvey rediscovered lost knowledge about the circulation of blood in our body, but his theories clashed with accepted understanding at the time and he was much criticized.

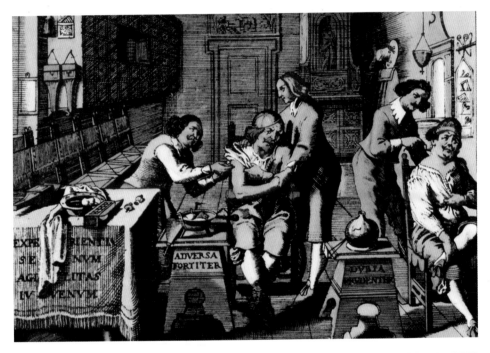

 A detail from a 10th century Flemish painting, showing a blood letting and other medical treatments.

Source B

Curious Cures of Old England,
Nigel Cawthorne, *Portrait Books, 2005*

"Nicholas Culpepper (1616–54) believed that a 'hot' liver, which produced sweet spittle and red urine, could be cured by bleeding the right arm."

Not many of the cures available were particularly pleasant, in fact many were disgusting. Potions and ointments made from herbs with strange names such as 'mandrake' and 'valerian' were commonly administered. Laxatives were often used to relieve many **ailments**. Serious wounds were treated with a special mixture, made by blending olive oil with a secret ingredient – cat! The flavour and goodness were infused into the potion by boiling the poor old moggie alive…

The condition we diagnose as depression had its own treatment too. Bizarrely, the cure was to pay for a pair of lamb's lungs to be placed on your forehead.

The dentist also had a number of good remedies to help you out. A patient complaining of toothache would be advised to down a strong syrup made from poppy seeds, and then the tooth decay that was causing the problem would be treated by an application of boiled frog.

The first of these might actually have helped relieve the pain, as the drug within poppy seed pods – opium – is well known as a pain reliever. Modern day dentists might disagree with the second 'cure' however!

Source C

A history website www.bbc.co.uk/history/british

Got a headache? Then rub your forehead with a rope that was used to hang a criminal. Suffer from rheumatism? Then wear the skin of a donkey. In pain with gout? Boil a red-haired dog in oil, add worms and the marrow from pig bones. Rub the mixture in. A painful liver? Drink a pint of ale every morning for a week – with nine head-lice drowned in it.

Are you bald? Use a shampoo made from the juice of crushed beetles. When the head is clean, rub in grease made from the fat of a dead fox. Are you a martyr to asthma? Swallow young frogs or live spiders – cover them in butter to help them slide down easier. Other crazy cures included powdered human skull, bone-marrow mixed with sweat, a stone that has killed a she-bear and fresh cream mixed with the blood of a black cat's tail.

The Great Plague

In Chapter 1 we saw how the Black Death swept across Medival Europe, leaving millions dead behind it. The bubonic plague continued to be a huge killer throughout this period, striking many times. The outbreak in London in 1563 and 1564 killed nearly 18,000 people and when the Great Plague struck again in 1665, approximately 69,000 people lost their lives. The disease spread quickly and with **devastating** effects.

The main method of preventing the spread of the deadly disease was to identify the infected houses with a red cross on white paper nailed to the door, accompanied by the sentence 'Lord have mercy upon us'. The houses were then to be sealed for a period of 40 days. Prevention was, on this occasion, no better than a cure. Both were equally unsuccessful.

Seeking a cure from the bubonic plague meant a terrifying visit from a plague doctor. Imagine waking up to be greeted by the vision of a tall, beaked figure, wearing a long leather coat and tall platform shoes. The 'beak' was part of a novel idea for keeping away the plague. The mask that covered the whole head was set with glass eye covers to protect the wearer. The beak was full of sweet smelling herbs that were meant to purify the 'foul air' that carried the plague. Plague doctors also carried a stick to beat away the plague victims if they attempted to get too close and, if possible, they attempted to cure the bubonic plague by bursting the buboes with a long needle called a **cautery**.

Bring out your dead!

Most people tried their hardest to stay away from people who had the bubonic plague, but one person who couldn't avoid contact was the 'searcher of the dead'. These workers were usually old women who were paid up to two pence per body that they identified as having the plague. Their job was to go into houses looking for signs of the disease and question the family. If plague was found, then the searcher had to record it. They were, however, open to bribery and some cases went unrecorded.

Deaths from diseases were recorded with the help of the searchers of the dead who assembled a written record. These written records were known as a 'bill of mortality'. Other diseases that were common at the time, and were also recorded, included **syphilis**, **scrofula** and **smallpox**.

Source D

Elizabeth's London,
Liza Picard, Phoenix, 2003

"Bubonic plague is basically a rodent disease. It strikes humans when infected fleas, failing to find a living rat once a flea host has been killed, pick a human instead. When the flea bites its new host, the bacillus enters the bloodstream."

This artist's impression of London at the time of the Great Plague is from a book published around 1900. Note the cross on the door at the left.

Other delightful diseases

One particularly nasty remedy for syphilis was to treat the symptoms with an ointment made from mercury, which would actually kill the patient!

It was believed that scrofula could be cured by being touched by the king or queen, although the more common cure was to have some blood drained off.

The front cover of a bill of mortality for London in 1664.

Source E

Medicine, *Paul Strathern*, Robinson, 2005

"*A grotesque and painful sexually – transmitted disease, syphilis was in some ways the Aids of the period from the Renaissance to the mid 20th-century. It was for centuries all but incurable. It could be passed on in the womb to the next generation, and in its final stage could result in the slow rotting of limb and brain prior to death.*"

Another illness, the 'sweating sickness', was very easy to diagnose – you sweated a lot and then died within a very short time period. In fact, it was so fast that you could complain about being hot and sweaty and be dead almost immediately. It is sometimes described as being like 'killer flu'.

Smallpox was a much feared and widespread disease. Queen Elizabeth I even bore the scars inflicted by it. One in three people at this time had faces that were covered in smallpox scars.

Discussion POINT ?

Do you think the bubonic plague could ever return?

Other common diseases included **measles, typhus, scurvy** and **malaria.** Many of the problems that we suffer from today existed then as well, but were simply not known or recognised. Measles is a good example. It can be easily spread, usually through coughs and sneezes, but also through contact. It is still a problem today, producing reddish-brown spots, and can kill. Typhus was spread by louse faeces that are scratched into the skin and then enter the bloodstream.

Although almost nothing was understood about these illnesses, there were some early attempts at caring for those with a mental illness. Patients were not cared for as well as they are today. The famous mental hospital in London called St Mary's of Bethlehem, or **Bedlam**, provided sanctuary for some. Commonly, the patient's head was shaved before admittance. Many poor beggars joined the mentally ill within the hospital walls.

Other hospitals also existed to treat patients with leprosy, although this disease has not been recorded in Britain since the mid-16th-century.

Stop the Clock

In 1671, a man called Thomas Blood stole the Crown Jewels.

BUZZ WORDZZ

Ailments
Autopsy
Bedlam
Cautery
Circulation
Devastating
Dissection
Malaria
Measles
Scarification
Scrofula
Scurvy
Smallpox
Syphilis
Typhus

A view of the interior of Bedlam, painted by the famous artist William Hogarth in 1735.

World Link

Ivan the Terrible was the first Tsar of Russia between 1547 and 1584.

To do task 1

Warm up...

a) What was scarification?

b) Describe the appearance of a plague doctor.

c) How is bubonic plague passed from person to person?

Some cures actually worked!

Despite the many inaccuracies and superstitions behind some of these medicines and cures, we today can still learn a lot from the methods of this time period. The Tudors and Stuarts were very good at using herbs and natural remedies to cure ailments, and we still make use of these today. Herbs like

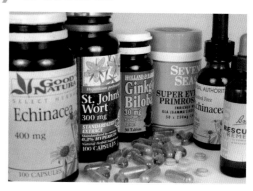

wormwood, valerian and lemon grass are all known to make people feel better. Earlier doctors may have had difficulty curing many diseases effectively but they were making progress towards finding cures. It was just slow progress.

After all, what chance did the scientists have against dangerous diseases that even modern day technologies have struggled to cure? In fact the threat of the plague still lingers on, even in modern society, as some people try to reproduce the killer strain and use it in 'germ' warfare. Luckily the scientists have also had their thinking caps on and have worked out what caused the plague, and how to combat it. Modern medicine means that it will never have such a devastating effect again!

To do task 2

Use your imagination...

Imagine that you are a Tudor doctor. Write your diary for a particularly busy day dealing with the sick. Remember to include details of the symptoms of the illnesses that you encountered, and what you wore. You may want to research the other illnesses, such as scurvy and malaria, to make your account really good.

Source F

www.channel4.com/ history/microsites/H/his tory/plague

In October 2001, the science journal Nature announced that the complete genetic structure of the bacilli responsible for the plague has been unravelled by scientists at the Sanger Centre in Cambridge (UK). This new knowledge will help in the search for treatments for the disease and to combat a possible weapon of bio-terrorism.

To do task 3

I'm a historian get me out of here...

Look back to pages 27 – 30 in Chapter 1 to remind yourself about the ways in which disease and illness were treated in the Middle Ages. Compare the two time periods. See if you can spot any changes and developments and list these using this table to guide you. You may even want to compare the methods to those of today.

	Middle Ages	Tudor and Stuart period
1		
2		
3		
4		

Will you marry me?

During this period, men and women could get married at a much younger age than now. The age of consent at one stage was very low – 14 years for boys and 12 years for girls. Although people could get married so young, it wasn't common. Marriage in a church was not compulsory, which meant that many went unrecorded.

It was a common belief in this period that women were both mentally and physically inferior to men. Women were seen as the weaker sex and their role in society became little more than a source of cheap labour. This was because women were being neglected in terms of what education was available. Virtually all lower-class women were unable to read or write. The role of a woman was definitely to work and get married. Unmarried women were frowned upon.

The trades and roles that women were employed in were varied but by no means always respectable. Many women had now begun to work in domestic service in the large households and, if they couldn't find work this way, they could turn to the textile trade or other manufacturing industries. Unfortunately, **prostitution** was another way of earning a living that some women were forced to resort to.

Cures for nagging women

Women who were seen as 'scolds' and nagged their husbands would often have to suffer the indignity of a scold's bridle. This was a sort of metal cage that fitted around the head, with a spike that pushed into the mouth and pressed down on the tongue, stopping the woman from talking. The poor lady would then be led around the town or village by a rope tied to the contraption, and humiliated in full view of all her neighbours. If this wasn't enough she could be ducked in a river using a device called a ducking stool, until she saw the error of her ways.

Some women did break away from the prejudice, however, managing to carve out careers as doctors and even surgeons, although this was rare.

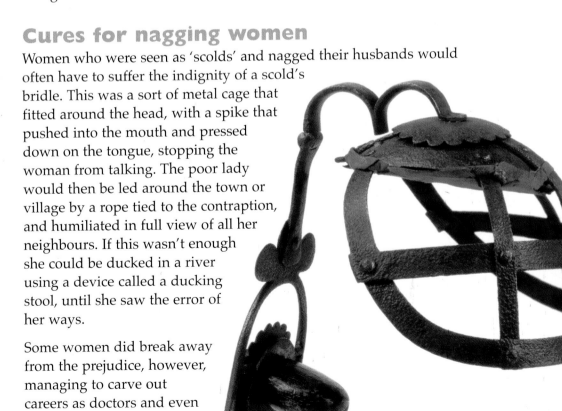

The position of women in society has changed remarkably in the last 100 years, but what did they have to put up with in Tudor and Stuart times?

- Were women equal to men in Tudor and Stuart society?
- Why did people believe in witches?
- Who was the infamous Matthew Hopkins and how was he a fraud?

NB...

The hatred of women is known as 'misogyny'.

Which witch is which witch?

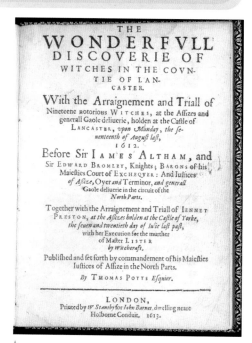

The title page of Thomas Potts' book detailing the trial of the Pendle Witches in 1612.

This feeling that women were inferior manifested itself in a more sinister way when women began to be accused of being witches. The stories of witches within communities have been around for centuries, captured in books such as *The Lancashire Witches* by William Harrison Ainsworth and *The Wonderful Discoverie of Witches* by Thomas Potts. The story of the Pendle Witches includes a famous account of the impact a witch trial could have on a local community.

The word 'witch' is derived from the **Anglo Saxon** word 'wicca' which means to bend or change. Witches were frequently identified as old women who had placed a curse on somebody, eventually resulting in an unfortunate event happening to that person.

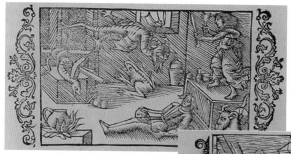

Source A

Witches and Ghosts of Pendle and the Ribble Valley,

Jacqueline Davitt, Tempus, 2006

"*One sort commonly said to be witches are women which are old, lame, blear eyed, foul and full of wrinkles. Poor sullen superstitious creatures in whose drowsy minds the Devil has a fine seat.*"

Images showing some of the things witches were supposed to be able to do.
Top left: Scandinavian witches calling up monsters while people were asleep.
Top right: Finnish witches selling wind to sailors.
Bottom left: Robbing graves and corpses for the ingredients of new spells.
Bottom right: Changing shape into animals.

During the reign of Charles I, a witch was said to have sat on a **crag** looking over the Burnley to Todmorden Road.

Source B

Witches and Ghosts of Pendle and the Ribble Valley,

Jacqueline Davitt, Tempus, 2006

*"One All Saints Day, a farmer called Giles Robinson was travelling along the route late at night after his business in town had taken him longer than he had anticipated. As he approached Eagle's **crag**, he heard an almighty crash in the air around him, and a fork of lightning hit the ground where he was just about to step. He looked up towards where the lightning had seemed to come from and saw the witch astride the rocky outcrop at the very summit of the crag. The lightning appeared to emanate from her up-stretched arms and the farmer watched, mesmerised by the sight, as heavy rain began to fall and the valley echoed with rumbling thunder."*

The Pendle Witches

In August 1612 ten people were executed for the crime of witchcraft in Pendle, Lancashire. The trial itself was recorded by the parish clerk, Thomas Potts, and so has become the source of much evidence for our knowledge about witchcraft in Britain at this time.

The witches had been accused of selling their souls to the Devil, gaining in return the power to kill or injure anyone they disliked. One of those convicted, Elizabeth Southerns, claimed they killed people by making a model of the victim – called a 'picture of clay' – which was then gradually crumbled or burned. The victim fell ill and soon died.

The traditional punishment for witches was hanging. However, the Scottish decided that it would be much better to burn them and make the witches pay for the service that they were providing, including the cost of the wood.

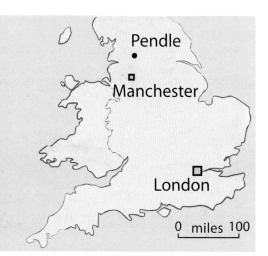

Map showing the location of Pendle, in Britain, the scene of one of the most famous witch trials in British history.

Source C

From the confession of Elizabeth Southerns,
describing how the spirit to whom she sold her soul – called Tibb – drank her blood

"The said spirit appeared unto her in the likeness of a brown dog, forcing himself to her knee, to get blood under her left arm and on awaking said "Jesus save my child" whereupon the dog vanished out of her sight, after which she was almost stark mad for the space of eight weeks."

Source D

Witches and Ghosts of Pendle and the Ribble Valley, *Jacqueline Davitt*, Tempus, 2006

"Demdike confessed to being a witch, claiming that the Devil had first come to her disguised as a boy named Tibb, who later changed into a dog, which sucked blood from her body for nourishment. She admitted killing a child whose father owed money to her daughter, then went on to describe how the quickest way of killing someone was to make a picture of clay, which should be pricked with thorns or pins and then burnt."

Discussion POINT?

Did witches ever exist or were they just made up? If so, why?

The real Ghostbuster!

BUZZ WORDZZ

Anglo Saxon
Crag
Depriving
Goatee
Persecution
Prosperous
Prostitution

One man in particular is linked with the **persecution** of women. The story of the 'Witch-finder General', Matthew Hopkins, is both interesting and intriguing and is often surrounded by confusion. Matthew Hopkins led a short but wealthy life in the east of England in the mid-1640s. He was the son of a vicar, although his father died when he was very young, and he came from a relatively **prosperous** family receiving a good standard of education. His motivation for catching witches was based purely around financial reward.

The belief that witches existed was strongest in this period, influenced by a fear of hell and the devil. More than one witch-finder patrolled the country seeking out their victims.

Hopkins was very good at his job. He used religion and people's religious beliefs to justify his campaign. He also claimed the support of Parliament, although it is unlikely that this was true. His fame spread by word of mouth, allowing him to build up his business. He was supported by a loyal group of helpers and followers and his technique was well practised and systematic.

He extracted confessions by using a number of different methods:

- **depriving** his victims of sleep.

- pricking his victims to see if they would bleed.

- torturing them.

- using the swimming test: if the witch floated it proved the water ejected them and so they must be guilty.

- looking out for a third nipple or 'teat' somewhere on the victim.

- looking for the presence of 'imps' – animals that were the servants of the devil who accompanied the witches.

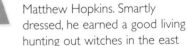
Matthew Hopkins. Smartly dressed, he earned a good living hunting out witches in the east of England.

The smartly-dressed Hopkins, who often wore a tall hat, long boots with spurs, a waistcoat and a cloak, was fair haired and had what we would call a **goatee** beard. Between 1644 and 1646, over 200 people were executed on account of the evidence that he provided. When he died, Hopkins was still in his twenties, high-lighting just how brief his career was!

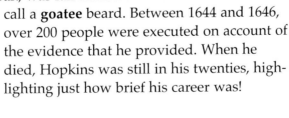

Witchcraft around the world

You would be wrong, though, if you believed that 'witch hunting' was a strictly British affair. It was widespread throughout Europe as well. Hopkins had been influenced strongly by the exploits of witch hunters in Belgium, Holland and Germany. Also, men were tried as 'Wizards' and 'Warlocks' so it wasn't just the women who had to fear for their lives.

Source E

Modern History,

J.M. Roberts. Duncan Baird Publishers 2007

In both Europe and North America there was an epidemic of witch hunting far more widespread than anything in the Middle Ages. Nor was this the end of superstition. The last English wizard was harried to his death by his neighbours well after 1700 and a Protestant Swiss was legally executed by his countrymen for witchcraft in 1782. The most famous example of witch trials in America are the Salem witch trials, in which Hopkins, according to some accounts, may also have been involved, although common sense and quality historical enquiry suggest differently. The Salem Witch trials lasted from 1692 to 1693."

To do task 1

Warm up...

a) What was the age of consent during this period?

b) Name two books about witches.

c) Give two ways in which Matthew Hopkins got his victims to confess.

To do task 2

Get creative...

Design an advert for the services of Matthew Hopkins. Include information about the methods used, his success rate and the area of the country that he worked in. Design the advert on plain paper and then age it by rubbing it all over with cotton wool soaked in cold tea. Remember, use only black ink as there were no coloured printing presses at that time.

In 1626, the Dutch founded New York.

Innocent women could easily have been accused of witchcraft during the Salem witch trials, particularly if someone had a grudge against them.

Why did people steal food?

For some people it was still a struggle to make ends meet, and they were forced to operate illegally just to put food on the table. Think about:

- what the term 'enclosure' means and the impact it had on everyday people's lives

- why people took personal risks to ensure there was something to eat.

Many people were left without a source of income and without access to natural stocks of fish and game. Rich farmers and landowners who planted the hedgerows that characterised enclosure, stopped people getting onto the land. Once again they made the class divide bigger and disadvantaged the common folk.

One way to overcome this divide – albeit illegally – was to poach. Poaching is illegal hunting or fishing on somebody else's land. At this time the ruling about hunting and fishing was something like this: if you had land worth £100 or more then you could hunt or fish on anybody else's land. But if your land was worth less than £100 then you couldn't hunt or fish anywhere else. Obviously this meant considerable problems for people who did not own land. Bad harvests added to the problem and people became even hungrier.

Local villagers made their way onto the land by the cover of darkness and hunted and fished in secrecy. Landowners employed game-keepers and used man-traps and 'body squeezers' to keep the common folk away. Occasionally, organised gangs of poachers were able to make large amounts of money through systematic poaching networks.

The Tudor and Stuart periods saw significant social change for the general everyday people of Britain. For years people had grazed, hunted and fished on the common land and rivers, but the Acts of Enclosure took much of this away from them.

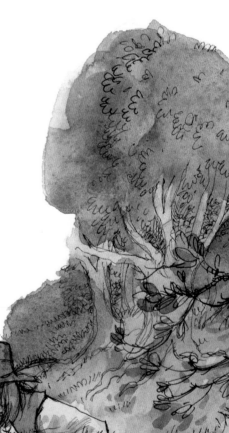

Discussion POINT?

As well as poaching there were other ways in which everyday people could operate outside of the law and overcome the rules of the rich and the laws of the land. What would you have done in their position?

Today, popular interest in pirates has probably never been greater, but what were their lives really like? Here we'll look at:

- Would ordinary people ever meet a pirate?
- What was a privateer?
- What was smuggling?

BUZZ WORDZZ

Circumnavigate
Exotic
Gibbets
Prosecute
Ruthless

Shiver me timbers!

The word 'pirate' comes from the Greek word 'peiran', which means to attempt or attack. Sometimes called 'Gentlemen of fortune' pirates profited from the huge increase in trade which had begun to flourish in the 16th and 17th centuries. In its simplest terms, piracy is robbery at sea. Pirates sometimes did trade by bartering for goods from other ships but in general, they made sea travel a risky business for merchant vessels. Favourite targets were ships carrying **exotic**, expensive goods such as silk and spices, in order to gain maximum profit. However, no ship was really safe from attack, as pirates needed basic supplies such as rope, tar, nails and even crewmates! The crew members were usually unpaid, working on a percentage of the sales of their takings.

Unless they were in the navy, most normal people would have had little, if any, contact with pirates. Their reputation in society was one of 'exciting adventurers' but, in reality, they were violent, brutal men – and very occasionally women – who thought nothing of committing violent crimes.

Tackling piracy

The British made it their mission to **prosecute** as many pirates as they possibly could during the 16th and 17th centuries. Pirates did appear in public on occasion, when on trial, which usually took place in London. As was common with public executions, thousands of people gathered to watch the show. Pirates were placed in **gibbets** (well-fitting iron cages), coated in tar, and often hung from strategic places along the river Thames. Before they were executed some pirates even made long speeches to the assembled crowds.

Privateers

Privateers were not pirates, although their tactics and behaviour were similar. They were often employed by countries that needed somebody to patrol their waters, but did not have a full-time naval fleet. These privateers were employed to capture the boats of the enemy. Privateers were **ruthless** men. Sir John Hawkins once accepted £40,000 to protect Spanish interests but, in truth, always stayed faithful to his queen, Elizabeth I. Another celebrated privateer was Sir Francis Drake – pictured alongside – famous for attacking and stealing from Spanish treasure ships. He is also famous for being the first Englishman to **circumnavigate** the globe in his ship, The Pelican.

Smugglers

Meeting a pirate was rare, but most people at the time would come close to smugglers who were often equally as evil. Smugglers took full advantage of the fact that, as an island, Britain has mile upon mile of unprotected coastline. These smugglers brought luxury goods such as tea, brandy and spices into the country without paying the import duties that the government imposed. This meant that they could sell the goods on cheaply.

People accepted this as normal, with local JPs and government officials often buying these goods. When challenged, the gangs could be violent and people who got in their way were sometimes murdered. One such gang to behave in this way was the Hawkhurst Gang – see source A.

This gibbet is preserved at a museum in Rye, Sussex. Alongside is a pillory, a common form of punisment for minor offences.

Stop the clock

The first English newspaper was printed in 1622.

An artist's impression of smugglers at work, unloading cargo in a secret cave. Smuggling began to decline during the mid-19th century.

▲ The steep path going up to the top of White Nothe in Dorset is believed to be a smuggler's path.

To do task 1

Extension...

Both piracy and smuggling still exist today.

Do some research on them and compare the reasons why people smuggle today, as well as what people smuggle.

Have the crimes changed much over the years?

Source A — HM Customs & Excise National Museum

"In the 1740s the Hawkhurst Gang, named after the Kent village, terrorised the south coast from Deal to Portsmouth. It was said that they could raise 500 men in an hour and they were prepared to murder to protect their trade. They even broke into the Poole Customs House to retrieve goods confiscated by the Customs Service. The gang's reign came to an end when its leaders were executed in 1748 and 1749."

Source B — Taken from Smuggling.co.uk/gazetter, a website on smugglers' Britain.

The smuggling beaches of east Sussex were largely controlled by highly-organised gangs; the Hawkhurst Gang was the most notorious. These "smuggling companies' were frequently based in coastal hamlets, but were as likely to conduct their business operations from an inland centre on the route to the main market in London.

The core gang members would thus not have been seamen, and farmed out the channel crossing to others – often local fishermen – or to French ships. As landsmen, the gang's talents lay in raising capital and arranging distribution.

Summary

All the crimes – and it is important to remember that they were crimes – have become the stuff of legend today for all the wrong reasons. However, some people who participated in these ventures did so purely for 'need' rather than greed. The poor were definitely not the most valued members of society and many laws were made that seriously disadvantaged anyone who was not wealthy and did not own land. So spare a thought for all those unfortunate men and women who were not actually criminals, but had to resort to crime to make ends meet.

Potato? What's a potato?

Food and drink in this period were similar to that of the Middle Ages. Some new foods were beginning to appear from overseas colonies though, the most obvious being the potato, which arrived from the West Indies in 1563.

Despite a number of poor harvests in this period, ordinary people could expect a reasonable standard of diet. The richer classes still had a fabulous diet, with meals full of indulgence, **extravagance** and luxury. Source A describes one **banquet** held by King Henry VIII.

In Chapter 1 we looked at the typical diet of Medieval people, with perhaps some surprises. Now we look at food and drink again, asking:

- Was food any better than in the Middle Ages?
- Did people have a good diet?
- What did people eat and drink in the Tudor and Stuart periods?

Source A

The Tudor Age, *Jasper Ridley*, Robinson, 2002

"There were eighty-two gold vases and fifty-two silver drinking cups on the tables, and during the supper servants entered, carrying a shaker 6ft long in solid silver, which threw wafers into the air for guests to catch and eat."

To do task 1

Use your imagination...

Imagine that you have been invited to a Tudor banquet. Describe what it was like and what you ate. Take time to describe the whole event.

Royal banquets were long and drawn out, often lasting over four hours and containing at least ten courses with huge amounts of food and drink being consumed. A rare sweet drink a – sort of liqueur called hypocras – was imported from the Levant and was a particular favourite with the royal family and those who could afford it. This sort of indulgence was a long way from what the majority could enjoy, but it shows how far trade had evolved by this time, allowing imports of specialist goods for a specialist market.

Source B

From the website www.pug.net

"...hypocras was primarily used during the issue de table, *the end of the meal and departure from the table. This generally consisted of things like cheese, candied fruits, light cakes. These items were thought to help close the stomach and start the process of digestion."*

The ordinary person might enjoy beef, mutton, lamb and pork, chicken and pigeons, puddings, pastries and all types of fruit and vegetables such as cabbages, peas, oranges, figs and cherries. All were available to buy from local merchants. Food was generally sweetened with lots of honey. Drink was not a problem, even though the quality of water was still poor. Ordinary people drank beer or ale and the rich generally drank wine.

The experience of dining at this time may have been slightly different to what you are used to today. When you sit down at the table to eat, you usually expect to use a knife, fork and spoon. In Tudor and Stuart dining areas there were very few knives and no forks. Spoons were available but most foods were eaten with fingers. By now, the poor could expect to eat off wooden plates, whilst the rich had the added luxury of pewter. The rich drank out of metal **goblets** as it was very rare to see glasses.

Seafood and fish were very popular amongst all of society. Salmon was still very easily caught in rivers such as the Thames and records even show a sturgeon being caught from the river in 1583. Even a few swordfish were occasionally available, along with all the common types of freshwater and saltwater fish.

Typical cutlery and tableware from the Tudor and Stuart period. Styling had evolved greatly since Medieval tools.

Water, water everywhere, but not a drop to drink!

Major rivers like the Thames were becoming increasingly muddy and **polluted**. Drinking river water was, therefore, increasingly dangerous. The main methods of ensuring adequate drinking water were:

- having it piped to your house

- paying somebody to collect it for you

- getting it from the water fountain or pump in the street.

The water pipes were often made from lead, which is poisonous. Also, because lead was a valuable metal, they were sometimes stolen. If not made from lead, they were hollowed out tree trunks that leaked and were porous, so they could not keep the water supply **uncontaminated**.

To do task 2
Get researching...
Many modern rivers, like the Thames, that used to be polluted are now enjoying a period of improvement. Try and find out what fish can be found in the River Thames today. Are they similar to the species that were around in the Tudor and Stuart periods?

Tudor kitchens

Preparing food and keeping it fresh were vital parts of daily life, although probably more time-consuming than they are for us today. Meat was usually salted or hung from beams in the house to age or cure, and most other foods were stored in barrels. Cooking was done over a wood or coal fire. Most of the time, food was cooked in iron or brass pots and **cauldrons**, which were hung over the fire.

Wealthier households may have had a variety of ways of cooking their food, the most famous of which was the **spit**. Large pieces of meat, or a number of different pieces, could be cooked all at once, although it was a slow process. The spit was turned by a 'spit boy', or later by their replacement the 'spit dog' that ran on a treadmill by the side of the fire. Delicate sauces were usually cooked on smaller, charcoal stoves.

BUZZ WORDZZ

Banquet
Cauldrons
Colonies
Extravagance
Goblets
Polluted
Spit
Uncontaminated

Source B

Discussion POINT ?

Why are birds like swan no longer eaten?

The Strange Laws of Old England,

Nigel Cawthorne, Piaktus, 2004

"Laws to curb excessive eating and drinking were also enacted by Edward IV and, of all people, Henry VIII. His sickly son Edward VI repealed them all, but to help the fishing industry, he passed a law banning the eating of meat on Fridays and Saturdays, and during Lent, except for the sick."

On 11 August 1587, the first potato was brought to England.

Eating out

The option to eat out was a very popular one. People were very keen to go to the local tavern and 'pub grub' was often very tasty and well prepared. Whole parties of people could be catered for, with the guests 'pre-booking' their table. One peculiarity was that those dining may have had to take their own knife with them as these sometimes weren't provided. Tables were often divided with a wooden partition, and the food, wine and ale flowed freely provided the diners kept paying for it.

Occasionally the whole affair got out of hand, resulting in an even livelier atmosphere and fighting. People often socialised with their friends at night time or during the day in these local taverns and, as our pubs are today, they were the centre of local life. People could go to these to watch entertainment, drink alcohol, smoke tobacco and meet members of the opposite sex.

For those of you who love food, you wouldn't have had a lot of fun during the reign of Edward III. He passed the 'Sumptuary Act', which made it illegal to eat more than two courses at a sitting, except on feast days.

There were many such laws that attempted to regulate things such as food, clothing or luxuries. There is little record of actually how effective any of them were in practical daily life!

To do task 3

Warm up...

a) What unusual drink did the royal family drink?

b) What type of fish was caught in the River Thames in 1583?

c) What was a 'spit boy'?

To do task 4

Challenge...

Compare the food enjoyed during this time period with the food enjoyed during the Middle Ages and the food that you eat today. Which foods feature in all three time periods? How have eating habits changed, and why? You will need to look back to Chapter 1 and think carefully. What similarities can you see?.

Cape Town was founded in 1652 by Jan Van Riebeeck.

There's nothing to do, I'm bored!

A wide and varied range of entertainment was available during this period. Some of it does not meet with what we today think of as entertainment. The one that best typifies the brutality of Tudor and Stuart entertainment is 'bear baiting'.

Source A **The Tudor Age,** *Jasper Ridley, Robinson, 2002*

"When the German traveller, Paul Hentzner, visited England in 1598, he attended a public bear baiting in London. After the usual baiting by the dogs, there followed another sport, whipping a blind bear. The bear, having been blinded, was fastened to a post by a chain. Five or six men then stood around the bear in a semi-circle with whips, 'which they exercise upon him without mercy, as he cannot escape from them because of the chain; he defends himself with all his force and skill, throwing down all who come within his reach, and are not active enough to get out of it, and tearing the whips out of their hands, and breaking them'. The proceedings sometimes ended with the torture of a pony; a monkey was tied to the pony's back, and dogs bit the pony's legs, while he desperately tried to shake off the monkey and the dogs."

Most people study Shakespeare at some stage of their school career, but to understand why he is seen as so important you need to know more about the time at which he lived and worked.

- Would you have enjoyed the entertainment available in the Tudor and Stuart periods?
- What was it like to watch a Shakespearean play?

Bears could be obtained quite easily because they still lived wild in the countryside. The job of **bearward** was a common one – basically they had to look after the bear. As the bear was very capable of defending itself, it was a fierce contest between the bear and the dogs that attacked it.

The tournaments made popular in the medieval period were still very well attended. Nobility competed and common folk observed. 'Riding at the ring' was still a popular part of these festivals.

Illegal games

This is a Shove Ha'penny board, and is a popular version of the Tudor game Shove Groat. Players aim to push the coin up the board so it falls exactly between the horizontal lines.

Nobles also still enjoyed sports such as hunting and hawking, and going to the theatre. Strangely, some games were banned in this period, and you might wonder why when many were nowhere near as violent as bear baiting – games such as skittles, tennis and bowls all faced the chop.

Gambling was very popular. The Tudors, whilst banning some games like 'Shove Groat' in 1541, also allowed others such as the first state lottery of 1569.

Football was the roughest game of them all. Some people even died whilst playing it. Football had been banned during the Middle Ages, but was now legal again. There was no limit on team size and no maximum pitch length – the pitch could be miles long. In fact, this lack of rules was typical of the whole game – anything was acceptable and both men and women played.

Loud, noisy and aggressive

Cockfighting was another rough and vicious sport. Events were widely publicised by the distributing of posters and handbills and large crowds gathered to see the event. Both birds were fitted with silver spurs on their legs and placed on a table, which had been covered with mats to prevent it getting damaged. Bets were placed and it was a fight to the death. Crowds were loud, noisy and aggressive.

English schoolboys during the Tudor and Stuart periods didn't always need to make up their own entertainment as they were allowed to take their own chickens into school with them, but only on **Shrove Tuesday**. These weren't normal chickens though, they were fighting birds or gamecocks. Public opinion on whether this was sport changed and this idea was banned in 1849.

To do task 1

Warm up....
a) What is 'bear baiting'?
b) Describe a game of football in this period.
c) Name three forms of entertainment of this period.

Other types of fun

The people of this time were actually very fortunate that they had so many different types of entertainment that they could enjoy. They could watch bull and bear baiting, pull the head off an unfortunate goose, attend a public execution, or play sports such as bowls and football. If this did not take their fancy they could listen to music, watch a play at the theatre and gamble in a tavern. Many types of gambling were popular, including card games, betting on sports, and board games. In fact, anything that a bet could be placed upon soon became sport for the locals. Betting was often organised on quite a large scale, with lotteries even making an appearance.

Source B

Elizabeth's London, *Liza Picard, Phoenix2003*

In 1567 a great lottery was held at London in St Paul's Churchyard, at the west door. The draw went on from 11th January to 1st May. The 400,000 tickets went on sale at 10s each, which was often shared between friends or by members of a livery company. The glittering first prize, as advertised, was the huge amount of £5000: £3000 in cash and the rest in armour, plate and household linens and hangings – which would not be much use to someone without a grand house to put them in.

Entertainment from far afield

Streets were sometimes filled with entertainers and curiosities which showmen had collected and proudly exhibited, including those brought back from newly discovered parts of the world. For the average citizen it cost a very small amount of money to witness something entirely new and unique. One diarist at the time recorded that, "It was said that a large live camel could be seen in a house on London bridge and Mr Cope, who had travelled in the Indies, sometimes showed visitors his collection, including the horn and tail of a rhinoceros, a unicorn's tail and flies which glow at night in Virginia instead of lights."

Discussion POINT ?

What types of entertainment during the Tudor and Stuart periods would have been your favourite?

The theatre

One form of entertainment that grew hugely in popularity was the theatre. Plays and recitals had long been popular but now new theatres were beginning to open. The Globe theatre (recently rebuilt in London) is a good example.

BUZZ WORDZZ

Bearward
Shrove Tuesday

Source B

Eyewitness Guide: Shakespeare,
Dorling Kindersley, 2006

"The popularity of the theatre in London attracted hostility from powerful enemies. The lord Mayor and his Aldermen saw any large gathering as a threat to law and order, and were always trying to close the playhouses down. Many city officials were also puritans, who were against any form of entertainment."

Source C

Eyewitness Guide: Shakespeare,
Dorling Kindersley, 2006

"Shakespeare sometimes had fun by making the boy players act the parts of women disguised as men. Rosalind, the heroine of *As you like it*, pretends to be a man called Ganymede. In disguise as Ganymede, Rosalind, who is in love with Orlando, offers to help him practise his wooing techniques by pretending to be the object of his affections – herself! So the boy playing Rosalind has to act as a woman, pretending to be a man, playing at being a woman."

No mention of the theatre in this period could be considered complete without the mention of one of the greatest names in theatre and literature – William Shakespeare. Born in Stratford Upon Avon in 1564, his father had been a glove maker and a member of Stratford town council. Despite being a country boy born and bred, Shakespeare went to London to begin his acting career. He became a member of the 'University Wits'.

The University Wits consisted of John Lyly, Thomas Lodge, Christopher

Some of the most well-known phrases and quotes actually come from Shakespeare's plays. Here's the opening lines of "All the world's a stage..." taken from *As You Like It*.

Shakespear's birthplace has been fully restored in Stratford Upon Avon.

The modern reconstruction of the Globe Theatre. It had been given special permission to have a thatched roof, which was the first time such a roof had been built in London since the Great Fire.

To do task 2
Get thinking...
What Shakespeare plays have you read or seen? Why do you think you still study him at school today?

Marlowe, Robert Greene and George Peeke. All these writers used 'blank verse', which consists of unrhymed lines of ten syllables. Shakespeare later joined a group called the 'Lord Chamberlain's Men', who performed at a theatre in London owned by a man called James Burbage. When this theatre had to be sold, it was dismantled and rebuilt in a new location across the river in 1598, and called 'The Globe'.

Most plays were acted out in the daytime, so that it was still light enough to see what was happening. There was music and even special effects using pulleys, ropes and trapdoors. There were, however, no women actors at all, just men, which meant that boys had to play the female roles.

Theatre lovers in England during the reign of King James I were handed a raw deal when the Plays Act of 1605 banned all plays that contained people mocking anything holy, like God. This became even more extreme though, because when Oliver Cromwell ruled over England the theatre was banned totally. (Not the only thing that Cromwell banned – he also banned Christmas and mince pies.)

To do task 3

I'm a historian get me out of here!

Good historians can compare differences and similarities between time periods. Look back to Chapter 1 and also think about what entertainment is like today. Write an analytical piece about the trends and similarities between the time periods.

To do task 4

Get thinking...

Imagine it's the 16th- century. The RSPCA has not yet been formed, but you are an early animal activist. Prepare a speech to give at a Tudor or Stuart fair, explaining what action you think should be taken against cruel sports, and why?

From *The tragical history of Doctor Faustus.*

The first African slaves were brought to America in 1619.

World Link

England's second greatest playwright?

One playwright and poet who has never received as much admiration as Shakespeare, but who may have been just as talented, is Christopher Marlowe. You may not have heard of such works as *The tragical history of Doctor Faustus*, or *The Passionate Shepherd*, but they were important pieces in their own right.

Marlowe may have disappeared into relative obscurity today, but his life in London was definitely not quiet and restrained. He was noted for his fantastically outrageous dress sense and he was one of the 'celebrities' of the time – often to be seen in various taverns and inns. He was also labelled a heretic when he criticised the new version of the Bible on its introduction to the church. Fittingly, it was in a pub that he met his maker, when he was stabbed in the eye over the bar bill! His death in 1593 left the way for Shakespeare to captivate us all for centuries.

A contemporary portrait of Christpher Marlowe.

Chapter 3

What was everyday life like for people during the Industrial Revolution?

Introduction

Your journey through the lives and experiences of everyday people began in the Middle Ages. Now we're almost 700 years further on, and entering a period generally known as The Industrial Revolution. The monarchs shown here all ruled in a period of huge change in British history, and these changes presented them with very particular problems to solve.

Who ruled ?

1760–1820
George III

1830–37
William IV

1820–30
George IV

1837–1901
Victoria

But, as you know by now, this book isn't about kings and queens, it's about ordinary people like you!

Read on to learn more about what life was like…

Our journey through time now takes us to the period that saw the birth of cities. So issues to consider are:

- How did living in the towns and cities change people's lives?
- Was life in the towns and cities improving?
- How were the poor looked after?

This painting shows the busy port of Liverpool at the turn of the 19th century.

Getting bigger and bigger

The growth of the British Empire had increased Britain's ability to trade with other nations. The trade from Britain was **predominantly** textiles, but trade of all types led to the growth of many British cities and ports.

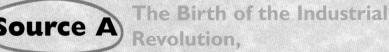

Source A — **The Birth of the Industrial Revolution,** *Kenneth Morgan,* Longman, 1999

"*By 1854–56 British exports had more than doubled from the figure half a century earlier, being worth £123,506,000.*"

The industrial cities were busy places, full of people, animals and carriages. Rich and poor lived side by side, but distinct differences were visible between the poor and rich areas. Streets, pavements and the fronts of houses showed the class of the area. It was the responsibility of the local authorities to maintain them, and the poorer areas, with less money, were therefore dirtier.

Streets were covered in a wide range of rubbish and waste, with **offal**, ash and **excrement** all **discarded** without a care. The contents of many chamber pots were thrown away outside the houses, which added to the foul appearance of the streets and, as the main method of transport in this period was still the horse, you can imagine just how much horse manure was on offer.

Keeping the streets tidy

Your parents may moan on occasion about the state of the streets, but the people who lived during the Industrial **Revolution** had nobody to blame but themselves. House owners were responsible for the pavement and lighting outside their own homes. This resulted in a street containing a number of different standards of cleanliness and up-keep.

Streets in the early part of this period were lit by lanterns and later by gas lights. Road surfaces were gradually getting better and by now were cobbled. Because the roads were so busy, it was not long before town councils began to build special roads that made their way around the edges of the main housing and trading areas, keeping the animals out of the way when they needed to be moved. Prior to this, towns had been blocked by animals being driven down the roads on their way to be sold at market or slaughtered.

Poor housing

Many of the houses occupied by the working classes were falling down around them. Lots of people lived in **slum** dwellings. These houses had none of the facilities that we take for granted today, such as running water and flushing toilets. Rooms were cold as no central heating was available, only a fire using coal or wood. Even windows were blocked up to avoid paying the window tax. Slum terraces were built in rows or around central 'courts', often sharing a **privy** and a water pump. Every floor of these houses or tenements was used, even the cellar. Animals also shared the facilities.

Source B

The Strange Laws of Old England,
Nigel Cawthorne,
Portrait, 2004

"An extra tax was imposed on windows. For houses with 7 windows, a tax of 2d a window was to be paid; 8 windows attracted 6d a window; 9 windows 8d a window; 10 windows 10d a window; 11 windows a shilling a window and so on up to 25 windows, which attracted a yearly sum of 2 shillings for every window."

▲ The bricked – up windows are evidence of window tax

◄ Working – class slums during the Industrial Revolution

Discussion POINT ?

Is it necessary to have windows in a house?

Getting bigger and bigger

Even at this relatively late stage in the history of Britain, there was still a large difference between the houses occupied by those with money and those without. In total contrast to the poor, the middle classes lived in more spacious residences and the rich, as always, lived in huge mansions. These houses were equipped with running water – often still piped through leaky water pipes made from elm or lead. Water pressure to pump the water through the pipes was achieved by way of water wheels such as Peter Moritz's (sometimes he is referred to as Peter Morice) water wheel in London, near London Bridge.

Source C

Dr Johnson's London,

Liza Picard, Phoenix Press, 2000

"Peter Moritz's water wheels under London Bridge had been turning since 1581. They were sophisticated pieces of machinery. Each wheel was 20ft in diameter, and rotated six times a minute at full tide. They were automatically raised or lowered according to the state of the tide. A reasonable pressure was achieved by pumping the water to a basin on top of a high tower of wood."

Night soil men.

Toilet facilities for all classes were still not up to much, although towards the end of the period they did progress to those with a flush. Cesspits were usually dug out by the 'night soil men' and, on occasion, the product of their efforts was sold as manure.

Blimey, what a stink!

Rubbish and human waste were dumped into rivers, washing it away. The rivers became so polluted that it sometimes looked as if it was possible to walk across them, so black and thick was the water. Pretty much any sort of human and animal waste was also thrown in. The rivers stank. In London, in the summer of 1858, the smell from the Thames got so bad that it was sickening. The stench was given the name 'The Great Stink'.

To do task 1
Get creative...

Design a campaign poster complaining about 'The Great Stink'. Include as many facts about why the stink has happened and how it can be stopped. Use your intelligence and your common sense, but don't include any references to modern technology.

BUZZ WORDZZ

Discarded
Excrement
Offal
Parishes
Predominantly
Privy
Slum
Squandered

The first copy of Dr Johnson's dictionary was printed in 1755.

Edwin Chadwick (1800 – 1890) tried to reform the Poor Laws and improve standards in public health.

The workhouses

How to control the poor was as much a problem in this period as it had been in Tudor and Stuart times. The **parishes** had control over the social welfare systems put into practice and corruption was obvious, with funds being embezzled and stolen. Workhouses had originally been established during the Tudor and Stuart periods and were now to be seen all across the country, enjoying a boom from 1722 onwards. They were meant to be for people who couldn't work due to a severe shortage of jobs, illness or disability. However, the people who genuinely could not find work were accompanied by those who simply did not want to work and this gave the genuine poor a bad reputation. This simply added to the belief of the upper classes that the poor were undeserving, had **squandered** their money and shouldn't be able to claim benefits.

Outdoor relief

As trade and industry boomed, workers from overseas came to Britain. A particular surge in immigrant labour from Ireland put extra strain on the social system and the system of poor relief based around the workhouses was inadequate. An alternative system was centred around money being offered to the unemployed, even if they did not enter the workhouses. This was called 'outdoor relief'.

The poor had to remain in the area where they were from, or were living, and had to wear a badge sewn on to the right shoulder of their clothing to indicate the area in which they should be claiming their money. Poor people often had so little money that even a proper funeral could not be afforded and they were buried with little dignity in pits or pauper's graves.

One of the most famous accounts of life in the workhouses was written by Charles Dickens in his novel 'Oliver Twist'. This classic work detailed the story of a young orphan who made his way from the workhouse to London to seek his fortune. At the start of the story Oliver is born into the workhouse where he faces terrible conditions.

Source C

Oliver Twist *Charles Dickens*

The room in which the boys were fed, was a large stone hall, with a copper at one end: out of which the master, dressed in an apron for the purpose, and assisted by one or two women, ladled the gruel at meal-times. Of this festive composition each boy had one porringer, and no more – except on occasions of great public rejoicing, when he had two ounces and a quarter of bread besides. The bowls never wanted washing. The boys polished them with their spoons till they shone again; and when they had performed this operation (which never took very long, the spoons being nearly as large as the bowls), they would sit staring at the copper…Boys have generally excellent appetites. Oliver Twist and his companions suffered the tortures of slow starvation for three months

In 1770, the east coast of Australia was claimed by Great Britain, courtesy of James Cook.

World Link

To do task 2

Warm up…
a) Describe the window tax.
b) What was 'The Great Stink' and when did it happen?
c) What was 'outdoor relief'?

The workhouses and the strict conditions within them were the result of a piece of legislation called the '1834 Poor Law Amendment Act'. This was an attempt to tackle the problems of the poor and the escalating costs of the poor rates. The man placed in charge of seeing that the legislation was enforced was Edwin Chadwick. The aim of the Act was largely to ensure that conditions in the workhouses were so dreadful that it would put people off entering them.

So harsh was the legislation that workers in the north of England rioted in protest.

To do task 3

Back to the future
We all take water for granted, but what do we know about it? Find out just how water gets to your house and what processes are involved. Compare today's water supply to that available during the Industrial Revolution.

The Andover Scandal
Stories of terrible conditions inside the workhouses soon appeared, one of the most famous being that of the 'Andover Scandal.' This was a shocking case showing the reality of how workhouses were run, and of the abuses people trapped in the workhouse system had to put up with. The Master of the Andover workhouse was known to starve the paupers living there, lock them in the mortuary as punishment and sexually abuse female paupers. After an enquiry by Parliament the Master was sacked and the Poor Law Board introduced in 1847, putting the system under closer official control.

To do task 4

Challenge…
These challenge tasks are getting harder now! Look back to the information on towns and living conditions in Chapters 1 and 2. Compare it to the information contained here. In your opinion, who had the better living conditions and why? Include as much evidence as you can to support your argument.

How far had the diet of everyday people improved since the Tudor and Stuart period? Let's look at:

- Was food during the Industrial Revolution any better?
- How did people buy their food and drink?

Food, glorious food!

Food, although widely available, still had to be bought, and the poorer classes could not afford food of a high quality. Bread formed the basis of their diet because it was cheap. The **cramped** conditions in their houses meant that cooking meals was not easy. Take-away food was the better option. Food, when bought, was regularly mixed with foreign bodies to increase the profit for those **rogue traders**. (See source A below)

The poor ate what they could get their hands on, including **tripe** (cow's stomach) and poor cuts of meat.

Discussion POINT ?

How long could you live eating mainly bread?

Source A — Dr Johnson's London,
Liza Picard, Phoenix Press, 2000

"The adulteration of food was a known scandal, but nothing was done to stop it. The Gentleman's magazine reported one case of a baker fined £5 for even possessing alum, but he must have been unlucky. As well as the pollution of bread, sulphuric acid was added to the vinegar, confectionery and pickles were coloured with copper salts, chalk came in handy again to thicken watered milk, lead was used to blacken tea and 'improve' wine, and if all this were not enough to cause severe intestinal distress, the acids in some food could react disastrously with the lead in lead-glazed pottery or pewter vessels."

Victorian shops

By the time Queen Victoria ruled, called the Victorian era and beginning in 1837, shopping was changing. Newer, more specialised shops were opening on the high streets and were attracting the middle and upper classes. The working classes generally shopped in 'general stores', which were smaller, or bought goods from markets, travelling salesmen and **hawkers**.

Most goods were not packaged but sold loose and could be bought from both markets and shops, and from mobile traders called **costermongers**, who pushed around a barrow containing fruit and vegetables. Prices were open to bargaining so many good deals could be found. Milk was bought from the 'cow dairy', which actually contained a herd of cows kept within the town or city. Once the railways had grown, this was replaced by milk brought in from the countryside.

New foods

Despite the fact that it was still easy for very odd things to find their way into various foods, the overall diet of everyday people was improving slowly. It might surprise you to know that ice cream was available as well as pies, pastries, pickled oysters, whelks and jellied eels. This take-away food was so readily available that it was generally preferred over home-cooked food, especially as it was unsafe to cook in your own home due to the serious risk of fire.

BUZZ WORDZZ

Costermongers
Cramped
Hawkers
Rogue traders
Tripe

A Victorian working-class market.

To do task 1

Warm up...

a) Give three ways in which food was tampered with.

b) Where could you buy your food during the Industrial Revolution?

c) What is a 'costermonger'?

To do task 2

Use your imagination...

You have been poisoned by some food that you have bought and have been asked to appear in court to testify. Write out your speech for the trial, including as much detail as you can about how you felt and what was wrong with the food. (Use examples from source A to help you.)

Stop the Clock

The first electric battery was made by Volta in 1800.

Getting an education was slowly becoming seen as more important.

Time to think about::

- Had schools changed since the Tudor and Stuart periods?
- Could ordinary people now get an education?

Stop the Clock

Jane Austen wrote *Pride and Prejudice* in 1813.

Come on – time for school

Until the Education Acts of the 1870s, 1880s and 1890s, schooling in the Industrial Revolution period was a hit and miss affair.

Source A

1870 – Possible for some children between the ages of five and ten to go to school.

1880 – All children between the ages of five and ten had to go to school.

1891 – All basic schooling now free.

In general, rich girls received a separate education in their own homes from a governess or tutor, although it was still believed that women did not need a good education as they would never need it to run a home and look after children.

Source B

History Without the Boring Bits,

Ian Crofton, Quercus, 2007

"In 1762 Lady Charlotte Finch became Governess to George III's children after the birth of the Prince of Wales. She is credited with having made one of the first known jigsaw puzzles, in the form of chopped up maps, which she used to teach the Royal children Geography."

Rich boys were sent to boarding school and boys from middle-class families went to grammar schools. Poorer children could go to a church school, set up by a charity. Here they would learn the basics – the '3Rs ' of reading, writing and arithmetic. Sunday school could also be attended, where children were taught about the Bible. Many children simply did not go to school because their families needed them to work and earn money. In the big cities, children could attend a 'ragged school' (pictured below) where work-related learning – making things and learning a trade – was combined with basic literacy and numeracy.

School life

School began at 9:00am and the school bell was rung by hand. Schools weren't much fun and the teachers were very strict. Misbehaving in class meant a beating and children who got too many answers wrong had to wear a 'dunce's hat'. A beating was usually in the form of being hit with a cane, or a leather strap called a 'tawse'. Skills were learnt using very modern technology – a slate, a globe and an abacus. Sentences and grammar were copied into what was known as a 'copy book'. Times tables would be chanted and simple arithmetic like fractions and decimals would be done on a slate. Playtime was fun though, with lots of games like marbles, football, skipping, hop-scotch and the hoop and stick.

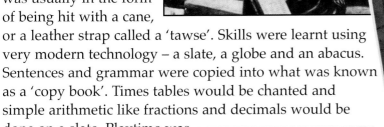

To do task 1

Warm up...

a)   Name three types of schools available during this period.

b)   What are the 3Rs?

c)   Name three games that were played at school.

To do task 2

Use your imagination...

Imagine you've just finished your first day at school during the Inustrial Revolution. Your mum has asked you to describe what your day was like. Write down what you would say in no less than 100 words.

To do task 3

Back to the future...

Schools and education have changed a lot over a short period of time. Using the table below to guide you, write down as many facts as you can about schooling during the Industrial Revolution and schooling today. What differences and similarities can you spot? You may even want to draw up a timetable for a school during the Industrial Revolution and compare it to your own.

Schooling during	
The Industrial Revolution	**Today**
1	
2	
3	
4	

The industrial Revolution was – as you can now tell – a period of great social change. That included advances in health and medicine:

- How healthy were people during the Industrial Revolution?
  - What medical advances had been made by this period?
    - Did medical advances have much impact on most people's lives?

Doctor, doctor!

Increasing medical knowledge and interest in healthcare led to new hospitals being founded during the Industrial Revolution, many of which were in London. These are some of the most well-known and famous hospitals in Britain:

- Westminster (1720).
- Guy's (1723).
- St George's (1734).
- The London (1740).
- The Middlesex (1745).

All these hospitals – set up at the start of the 18th century – now functioned alongside the hospitals that had been founded in earlier years: St Bartholomew's, St Thomas' and St Mary's of Bethlehem. Specialist hospitals for other illnesses and medical issues were now being built – smallpox and maternity hospitals are prime examples. Hospital care became a more important need because of the Industrial Revolution.

Typhus

Many diseases were common within the towns and cities, one of which was typhus. Typhus reached a peak in the 18th and 19th centuries, but had begun to decline by around 1850. It is often called 'gaol fever', 'Irish fever' or 'spotted fever'. The disease is passed on through lice. When conditions within a community are unclean and overcrowded it is very easy to catch, especially in winter. Within two weeks of being exposed to the disease it will have an effect on the body.

Cholera

Cholera was a huge problem in industrial cities because of the general overcrowding, poor hygiene and lack of knowledge about how certain diseases spread. In 1832 alone, 20,000 people died from the disease, with the worst outbreaks occurring between 1848 and 1853. Cholera is caused by a **bacterium** called 'vibrio cholera'. It leads to a few unpleasant symptoms, such as watery diarrhoea, stomach cramps, dehydration and poo that smells of fish! It can be cured by drinking plenty of fluids and replacing any salts and minerals that have been lost due to dehydration.

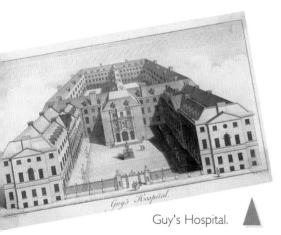

Guy's Hospital.

Medical advances

Smallpox was another great health problem at this time, and affected thousands of people. The disease was only brought under control after the pioneering work of one man, Edward Jenner. Jenner, pictured here, believed that smallpox could be cured and, through his observations, he deduced that milkmaids who had suffered from cowpox (a disease affecting cows) did not get smallpox. He suggested that this was because there was a similarity between smallpox and cowpox, and that cowpox gave some protection against smallpox.

In May 1776, Jenner tried to prove that he was right by injecting a young boy, James Phipps, with a sample from a cowpox blister. After a short period, he gave the boy the smallpox **virus**, but the boy did not get the disease. Jenner was right. He named the solution to the smallpox problem a **vaccine** as he used the Latin word for cow, which is 'vacca'.

Jenner did not get rich from his discovery, in fact, he refused any financial reward at all. By the start of the 20th century, smallpox was no longer a problem in any developed nation. (Jenner is also credited with the discovery of **angina**, a disease affecting the heart.)

Source C

England the Autobiography,
John Lewis-Stempel (ed.), Penguin, 2006

"A number of children were inoculated in succession, one from the other; and after several months had elapsed, they were exposed to the infection of the Small Pox; some by Inoculation, others by various effluvia and some in both ways; but they all resisted it."

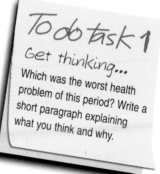

To do task 1
Get thinking...
Which was the worst health problem of this period? Write a short paragraph explaining what you think and why.

Burke and Hare

As the Victorians improved medical knowledge, they did so based on scientific principles including the **dissection** of bodies to find out more about the way they worked. The need for bodies to help with pioneering research prompted an unusual crime – body snatching. Two criminals most notorious for this were 'Burke and Hare'. Burke ran a cheap boarding house and he used this to get his victims – he killed his customers! The bodies were then sold on to Robert Knox, a surgeon, who paid between £8 and £14 per body.

Left: William Burke;
Right: William Hare.

Anaesthetics

Advances were also being made at this time with **anaesthetics**, reducing the amount of pain that a patient had to endure during an operation.

Source B

Victorian Jobs, *Brenda Williams, Heinenmann, 2003*

"In 1846, a surgeon named Robert Liston gave a patient a drug called 'Ether', to make him unconscious, before cutting off his leg. The patient woke up when it was all over, asking when the surgeon would start. He had just had the first operation in Britain under a general anaesthetic."

It's a baby!

In the previous chapters you've seen numerous descriptions of the ongoing problem that childbirth posed for people. It was in the Industrial Revolution period that significant improvements were finally made, giving women a better survival rate. A Scotsman named William Smellie, pictured here, pioneered **midwifery** in the 1750s, publishing a book in 1752.

Prior to the impact of these modern midwifery techniques, people relied on superstition and the power of religious relics and artefacts to make the birthing process go smoothly. People even believed that laying relics on the pregnant woman's stomach during labour would help! Babies who were in an unusual position in the womb would often die during birth as the whole process was delayed, starving the baby of oxygen, often resulting in the death of the mother as well.

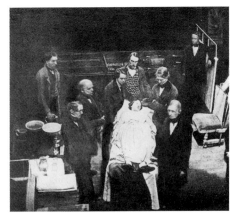

One of the first operations using ether as an anaesthetic took place in Massachussetts, USA in 1897.

Source C

Medicine, *Paul Strathern, Robinson, 2005*

"He advocated that women should where possible give birth in airy rooms illuminated by daylight. Newborn infants should not be wrapped up in swaddling clothes, but should be allowed free movement which would allow the limbs to develop and give strength to the bones. He also encouraged breastfeeding as a natural process which helped the mother and child to bond. Smellie introduced the measurement of the pelvis, as well as attempting to measure the foetal cranium in utero (within the uterus, or in the womb). He is also responsible for the first public introduction of an improved forceps to assist difficult births."

The Victorians and death

The Victorians were far more familiar with dealing with death than we are today, finding the whole experience much more enjoyable. Death was celebrated and the funeral was an important and significant event. Some people even made their own funeral preparations before they had actually died.

People lived much shorter lives and a belief in God and the afterlife was extremely important.

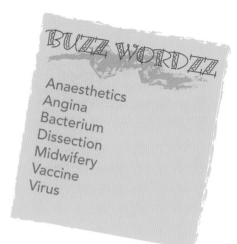

BUZZ WORDZZ

Anaesthetics
Angina
Bacterium
Dissection
Midwifery
Vaccine
Virus

Source D

The Victorian Undertaker,
Trevor May, Shire Publications, 1997

"The actress Sarah Bernhardt kept her coffin in her boudoir and was photographed in it and some men, being of a frugal nature, who had obtained their coffins in advance, used it for the time being as an upright cupboard in their homes."

A lavish Victorian funeral.

Source E

The Victorian Undertaker,
Trevor May, Shire Publications, 1997

"The greatest festival of all is perhaps the funeral. The poverty of the family makes no difference to their eagerness, and the little nest-egg which a man has provided to help his wife through the first months of widowment is often lavished within a few days of his death. I have known a woman have a hearse with four horses, and a carriage for her husband's funeral, and within two weeks apply to the Guardians to feed her children."

Stop the clock

The home of the 'Elgin Marbles' was changed from Athens to London in 1801.

To do task 2

Warm up...

a) What is typhus?

b) Who did Burke and Hare sell bodies to?

c) What disease did Edward Jenner develop a cure for?

To do task 3

Get creative...

Design a leaflet or poster about typhus that would have helped conrol it in an industrial city in the mid –19th-century. Include both facts and pictures helping people to identify the disease and avoid it in the future. If you don't think every-one can read, how else might you get them to understand your message?

To do task 4

Back to the future...

Find out what vaccinations are available today. What vaccinations have you had and at what age did you have them? You may need some help with this. Remember, you have Jenner to thank for your good health!

Life as a Victorian undertaker

However, no matter what lengths the ordinary people went to in their quest for a grand passage into the afterlife, they couldn't compete with the funerals arranged for the aristocracy and the monarchy. Wellington's funeral in 1852 was like nothing ever seen before.

Source F

From the website of St Paul's Cathedral. www.stpauls.co.uk

The state funeral of Arthur Wellesley, 1st Duke of Wellington (1769-1852), was the first large-scale service of its kind to take place under the Dome of the Cathedral. The building was closed for almost six weeks, whilst extra tiers of seating and grandstands were erected in the aisles and transepts in preparation for the 13,000 attending; heavy black cloth was hung at the windows; daylight was virtually excluded, the Dome being illuminated only by a corona of gas lights under the Whispering Gallery. Members of government and university predominated in the congregation.

The choir was augmented for the occasion to 80 men and 40 boys with 40 additional singers and instrumental performers; the organist, John Goss, composed music to mark the occasion. The start of the Prayer Book burial service was delayed by almost an hour on account of the late arrival of the coffin; the end was marked with the lowering of the Duke's coffin through the floor of the Cathedral into the Crypt. Wellington's tomb with its sarcophagus of Cornish porphyry was not finished for another five years. The twelve-ton funeral carriage which carried the coffin, together with model horses, was re-erected at the West end of the Crypt in 1855; it remained on view at the Cathedral until the early 1980s when it was removed to Stratfield Saye (the family seat). A miniature paper model is still on display in the Cathedral Library.

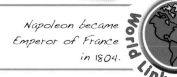

Napoleon became Emperor of France in 1804.

World Link

Come on, we're going out!

Although for much of this period, nice, friendly entertainment is what most people wanted to see, all sorts of people were catered for. There was a wide variety of entertainment available, much of which was good, wholesome, family fun, but there was also no shortage of more daring materials. Burlesque – a form of striptease combined with comedy – and other striptease were popular, but this was as far as it went. Respectability was the key and people flocked to see circuses, ventriloquists, comic operas and plays. Colourful posters and flyers drew the punters in and the theatres and music halls were packed to the rafters, with both serious plays and pantomimes being very well received. Animals from exotic countries were exhibited in travelling menageries, the most famous of which was owned by George Wombwell and opened in 1805.

Wombwell's menagerie

Wombwell's **menagerie** was a very popular travelling display of animals. Collections of wild animals always attracted a lot of spectators; even Queen Victoria enjoyed private performances. It was first exhibited in 1807. George Wombwell had started his show with only two snakes and then built up a huge collection of animals. A band played and drew the crowds in and the beast wagons containing the animals were hidden behind screens covered in fantastic drawings and decorations.

There were now all sorts of things people could do to fill their spare time:

- How had entertainment changed by this period?
- Was the entertainment genuinely entertaining?
- What did people do with their leisure time?

George Wombwell. On his death in 1850 newspapers nationwide printed his obituary, so well was he known in Britain.

Source C

The True History of the Elephant Man,
Michael Howell and Peter Ford, Allison & Busby, 2006

"I could never sufficiently admire the gorgeously uniformed bandsmen, whose brazen instruments brayed and blared from noon till night on the exterior platform, and the immense pictures, suspended from lofty poles, of elephants and giraffes, lions and tigers, zebras, boa constrictors, and whatever else was most wonderful."

One thing these audiences loved was variety. Varied shows packed full of a huge array of entertainment types were just what the paying public wanted. Travelling 'freak shows' and displays of oddities were also popular. In fact they were so popular that many people were unknowingly conned by fake displays of curiosities, mixed in with a few genuine attractions.

All the attractions or acts described here were enjoyed by many thousands of people.

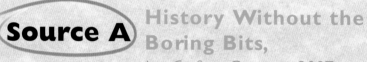

Source A History Without the Boring Bits,
Ian Crofton, Quercus, 2007

"In 1825 a Mermaid was exhibited at Bartholomew's Fair, London. It turned out to consist of the dried head and body of a monkey and the tail of a fish."

Julia Pastrana (the Ape Woman)

Julia arrived in London in 1857 and by this time she was already a well-travelled entertainer. She was born in Mexico, with an unfortunate condition – she was hirsute, which basically means that she was very hairy. In fact, she was covered in hair so thick that claims were made that she was related to both bears and monkeys. Advertised as the 'Ape Woman' or the 'nondescript,' she was actually a very intelligent woman who formed a successful partnership with her husband. Everywhere she was exhibited crowds flocked to see her in great numbers. Even when her untimely death cut her 'live' act short, her husband had her carefully embalmed and he exhibited her in a glass case.

The Elephant Man

The Elephant Man (whose real name was Joseph – sometimes John – Merrick) was exhibited in a few different travelling curiosity shows in the 1880s. Merrick believed that his illness came from an unfortunate accident when his mother had allegedly been knocked down and frightened by an elephant. This is untrue and scientists now believe his deformity may be linked to neurofibromatosis or, just as likely, Proteus syndrome. Many people think that he was exploited, but he had actually volunteered himself for 'show business' where other employment opportunities proved to be unsuitable for him. Merrick was an unusual exhibit, although the type of show that he was a part of was not. In Victorian England it was common.

The Elephant Man was eventually rescued from show business and spent the rest of his life in the London Hospital.

Julia Pastrana, also known as the Ape Woman.

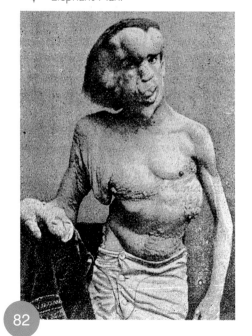

Joseph Merrick, also known as the Elephant Man.

Source B

The True History of the Elephant Man,
Michael Howell and Peter Ford, Allison & Busby, 2006

"…especially on Saturday nights, to see dwarfs, giants, fat women and monstrosities at the freak shows. There was a freak museum at a public house – The Bell and Mackerel, near the London hospital. It was on one of these visits in 1884 I saw 'on show' opposite the London hospital a repulsive human being known as the Elephant Man. The poor fellow John Merrick was deformed in body, face, head and limbs. His skin, thick and pendulous, hung in folds and resembled the hide of an elephant – hence his show name."

Madam Tussaud's waxworks

Tussaud's current building in London was built in 1884, 34 years after the lady herself had died. Her fame increased throughout her lifetime after her arrival in England in 1802. Anna Marie Tussaud – shown alongside here – was a very talented artist who had turned her hand to waxworks during the French Revolution. Her display of portraits of famous people modelled from wax soon became a huge hit. Waxworks had long been enjoyed at fairgrounds, but Tussaud's were a different class, allowing famous events and people to be seen (in wax) by ordinary people.

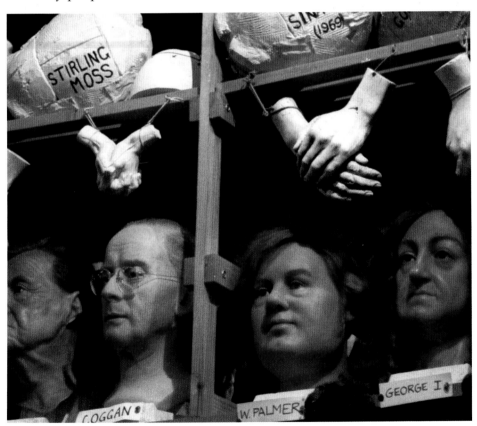

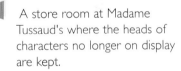
 A store room at Madame Tussaud's where the heads of characters no longer on display are kept.

Source D — 'Madam Tussaud', Kate Berridge, Punch magazine 1849, John Murray, 2006

"In these days no one can be considered properly popular unless he is admitted into the company of Madame Tussaud's celebrities in Baker Street. The only way in which a powerful and lasting impression can be made on the public mind is through the medium of wax. You must be a doll at Madame Tussaud's before you can become an i-dol(l) of the multitude. Madam Tussaud has become in fact the only dispenser of permanent reputation."

Maddam Tussaud's is still an incredibly popular tourist attraction today. Wayne Rooney a favourite waxwork, is shown here.

Barnum

American showman P. T. Barnum exhibited General Tom Thumb (Charles Sherwood Stratton) in England. Tom Thumb was a very small man, a man in miniature. In fact, Stratton was not a fully-grown man, rather a very small young boy, who looked older than he was. One of his biggest fans was Queen Victoria. His exhibitor, Barnum, was a very successful businessman from America and was very wealthy. He had at one stage even tried to purchase Madam Tussaud's exhibition.

Source E

The life of P. T. Barnum,

P.T. Barnum, University of Illinois Press, 2000

"Not to have seen General Tom Thumb was voted to be decidedly unfashionable, and from the 20th of March until the 20th July (1844) the levées of the little General at Egyptian Hall were continually crowded – the receipts averaging during the whole period about $300 per day, sometimes quite considerably beyond that."

Charles Sherwood Stratton, also known as General Tom Thumb.

Buffalo Bill

Buffalo Bill, otherwise known as William Frederick Cody, brought his Wild West show to England towards the end of the 19th century. Buffalo Bill was first seen in Britain in 1887 when he came over to mark the **Golden Jubilee** of Queen Victoria. At his show in 1887 at Earl's Court, in the crowd sat Queen Victoria. His show contained magnificent displays, with people able to watch Indians attacking cowboys, sharp shooters like Annie Oakley and wild buffaloes and elks.

Posters advertising Buffalo Bill's Wild West shows.

His show – called 'Buffalo Bill's Wild West and Congress of Rough Riders of the World Show' – was exciting entertainment on a big scale. The cast of 200 included real-life cowboys, native Americans, broncos and even buffalo. The show was performed every night for five months in what was the biggest indoor arena ever constructed in Western Europe. Incredibly many of Bill's cast were recreating the battles they had actually fought in just a few years earlier – and some people involved were genuine outlaws on the run from the US military!

Even more incredible is that when Bill decided to take his show back to the US, one member decided to stay and settle in Manchester. Charging Thunder – a red Lakota chief of the Sioux Nation – married one of the show's American horse trainers. He was offered a job at the local circus, although the authorities made him change his name to the much more English-sounding George Edward. He died from pneumonia in 1929 at the age of 52 and his body is buried in Manchester's Gorton Cemetery, albeit with his English name on the tombstone.

BUZZ WORDZZ

Burlesque
Hirsute
Menagerie
Golden Jubilee
Thaumatrope discs

The Great Exhibition

The Great Exhibition was a display of everything there was to celebrate about the British Empire. It was opened by Queen Victoria on 1 May 1851. The exhibition was housed in a fantastic glass building that had been built especially for the occasion called The Crystal Palace. The building covered an impressive 19 acres and contained a massive 294,000 glass panes.

Source F — **England the Autobiography,** *John Lewis Stempel (ed.), Penguin, 2006*

"Whatever human industry has created you find there, from the great compartments filled with railway engines and boilers, with mill machinery in full work, with splendid carriages of all kinds, with harness of every description, to the glass – covered and velvet spread stands loaded with the most gorgeous work of the goldsmith and silversmith, and the carefully guarded caskets full of real diamonds and pearls worth hundreds of thousands of pounds."

500,000 people watched the Queen open the exhibition in Hyde Park. During the six months that the exhibition remained open, 6,000,000 people visited it, including Queen Victoria, who came through the doors every two days on average. At the centre of the exhibition was the fabulous 'Koh-i-noor' diamond. The Crystal Palace itself was moved to Sydenham, South London after the Great Exhibition had closed and was rebuilt on the new site. It was officially reopened on 10 June 1854.

NB...

The famed Koh-i-noor diamond now forms part of the Crown Jewels and has done ever since the Great Exhibition. However there has recently been a claim made by the original Indian owners of the diamond for it to be returned to them!

To do task 1

Get creative...

You have been asked to produce a 3 minute TV feature on the Great Exhibition. What particular aspects are you going to focus on? How was it built? What was the variety of attractions on display? When you've decided, create a storyboard outline of the programme and list where you will get the background information from.

Stop the Clock

Faraday first demonstrated electricity in 1831.

Crystal Palace ▶

OPENING OF THE GREAT EXHIBITION, MAY, 1, 1851.

Entertainment was by now so varied that you could do something different every day of the year. One event that always captured the imagination was the balloon ascent. This stunt, which usually involved a man dangling from a hot air balloon, was truly death – defying in fact, the occupant of the balloon was sometimes killed when the stunt went wrong.

De Groof, the Flying Man.

Source G

Victorian Entertainment,
Alan Delgado, David and Charles, 1971

"[De Groof] …constructed a 12ft stand suspended some 30ft from the balloon. From this stand he manipulated monster wings some 37ft long, and a tail 18ft long. At the first attempt he landed safely at Brandon in Essex, but in July 1874, when he repeated the experiment, it ended in disaster."

Going to the pictures

We may think of the cinema as a very modern invention, but it dates back to the late 19th century. Moving images produced by 'magic lanterns' and panoramas that moved around the audience were all the rage before the 'motion picture' itself arrived to entertain the public. If a trip to this was not possible, **thaumatrope discs** and hand shadows had to do. A thaumatrope disc is a disc with an illustration on each side. When spun, the two images combine to create what looks like a moving image, caused by the way in which the two images flash quickly. The spinning of the disc is created by a string on each side of the disc that is wound up and then released.

A thaumatrope show.

Fig. 50. — Lanterne magique.

Street entertainers were always a regular sight – Punch and Judy men, organ grinders with their monkeys, bands, people on stilts and donkey rides were all popular, as were photographers and parades.

Victorian theatre

For the Victorians, the 'music hall' was a hugely popular form of entertainment – it was a form of variety show with singing, dancing, storytelling, and much more. One of its most well-known stars was Marie Lloyd.

Music-hall favourite Marie Lloyd (1870 – 1922) enjoyed enormous success on the stage but had a troubled personal life.

Source H From the website www.peopleplayuk.org

"Known as the 'Queen of the Music Hall' Marie Lloyd's career spanned forty years. She first appeared at the Eagle Tavern in London aged 15 as Bella Delmare, singing 'My Soldier Laddie'. By 1885 she had become Marie Lloyd with her hit song 'The Boy I love is Up in the Gallery'. She was a huge success and topped the bill at the West End music halls.

Marie Lloyd's songs were full of innuendo and double meaning: 'She'd never had her ticket punched before' and 'Oh Mr Porter what shall I do' appear to be innocent on first reading but could take on a very saucy interpretation when sung by Ms Lloyd.

To do task 2

Warm up...

a) What was Julia Pastrana also known as?

b) What is a menagerie?

c) Who was Charles Sherwood Stratton?

d) When did the Great Exhibition open?

e) Name three sports that the Victorians enjoyed.

The Victorians and sport

Sports that we enjoy today, such as cricket, horse racing, boxing and road running, were becoming much more popular at this time. Sport had also made the leap from local to national scale and professional sport and sportsmen were appearing, such as the cricketer W. G. Grace.

The national growth in interest in the 'new' sports was still slow, and certain areas of the country lagged behind others. As is the case today, people loved to watch sport, and gradually more and more people wanted to play it. The richer middle classes could now add cricket, fishing, horse racing and rowing, to their leisure interests. This opportunity to do more with their leisure time came about after laws had been passed to reduce the number of hours that people worked. More time at the weekend meant more time for relaxation and sport.

The cruel sports that were so popular hundreds of years before – like bear and badger baiting and cockfighting – were now declining in popularity. Laws to protect animals had been passed and societies like the RSPCA had been founded. People were now beginning to care more about the welfare of animals.

WG Grace – refered to as 'the best-known Englishman of his time' – did more than anyone to popularise cricket.

Henley rowing regatta photographed around 1900.

In 1807, the importation of slaves was banned in America.

World Link

A Victorian bathing machine.

Source H

Robert Louis Stevenson

"When I was down beside the sea,

A wooden spade they gave to me,

To dig the sandy shore,

My holes were empty like a cup.

In every hole the sea came up.

Till it could come no more."

Oh, I do like to be beside the seaside!

Days out and holidays at the seaside resorts were gaining in popularity, with trips available on the railways and by boat. The Victorians loved going to the seaside and everything that it involved. All classes of society could be catered for, with expensive hotels and cheap boarding houses all taking guests. New, expensive piers had been built to cater for the holidaymakers. Mixed bathing was frowned upon, but modesty could be kept safe by changing in a bathing machine on wheels that could be pushed down to the edge of the water.

Blackpool Toower was built between 1891 and 1894 and is 158m high. Painting it takes seven years to complete and its maintenance workers are known as *Stick Men*.

A day at the seaside wasn't quite the relaxed time that we know today. For a start, everyday clothing wasn't as airy or as comfortable, with suits and long heavy dresses being worn to walk along the promenade. Even the swimming costumes were very formal, with long sleeves and legs.

Despite this, some people did break the rules: the first nudist beach was in Abergele in 1794!

Entertainment at the seaside was easy to find, ranging from making sandcastles with a bucket and spade, through to Punch and Judy shows and paddle boats. In fact, there was so much entertainment that it was impossible to get bored. People were busy eating whelks and jellied eels and ice-cream, and attending all the funfairs and variety shows.

A Victorian seaside pier.

To do task 3

Get thinking...

You are a talent agent working during the Industrial Revolution. You need to employ an entertainer. Say who you will choose and why. Design a poster to advertise them to accompany your decision.

To do task 4

Back to the future...

Variety is back in the public eye. People don't want the same type of entertainment all the time. Think about the most entertaining show or night out you have ever been to and write a short piece about it. What did you like about it, and why?

Have you heard the expression 'to break into a sweat'? It actually relates to types of work common in the Industrial Revolution.

- What new jobs were now available?
  - What is a 'sweated trade'?
  - Were there any changes in types of employment available?

It's off to work we go!

The Victorian era saw a new pattern in the way people could live and work. Transport improved to the point that people could now live outside the city, but still work in the city. They commuted on new forms of transport like the **omnibus**, first pioneered by George Shillibeer in 1829. Literally translated from Latin, 'omnibus' means 'for all'. Each day people commuted between work and home, and this was an innovation in the way British people lived and worked.

Victorian offices were nowhere near as technologically advanced as ours are today. Both electricity and the telephone were not invented until the 1880s, and the main ways of communication was via an errand boy, by telegraph – which was invented in the 1840s – and by post using the 'Penny postage' system. Letter writing was done by hand with quill pens that had metal nibs but in the 1870s the invention of the typewriter offered a new and quicker alternative to handwritten letters.

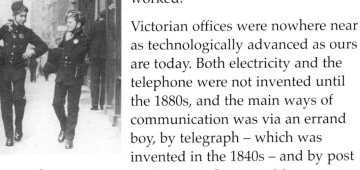

Telegram boys on the streets of London in the 1930s.

A Penny Black stamp, circa 1840.

Discussion POINT ?

How do forms of communication today differ from the Vicrorian forms described here?

Source A

Victorian Jobs, *Brenda Williams, Heinemann, 2003*

"Wages were paid in pounds, shillings (s) and pence (d). A typical working man in the 1840s might earn about 15 shillings (75p in today's money) a week. He would spend about 3 shillings and sixpence (17p) each week on bread and about 2 shillings and sixpence (12p) on rent."

Sweated trades

Not everybody was lucky enough to work in an office though. Many people who were desperate for work could earn a very small amount of money by working in a sweated trade. The business was run by a 'sweater' who then allocated the work to different people.

Source B

Victorian Jobs, *Brenda Williams*, Heinemann, 2003

"Sweated workers made straw hats in Luton, cut leather for shoes in Northampton and finished wooden penholders in Birmingham. In the 1890s, one Birmingham woman reported that she earned less than 2 pennies (1p) for making 144 penholders. Each penholder was rubbed smooth with sandpaper and then given five coats of varnish with a sponge."

The Metropolitan Police force was set up in 1829.

Chimney sweeps

One of the most unfortunate workers was the chimney sweep. Coal fires were the only source of heating for most homes, and so demand for chimney sweeping was high. Sweeps were usually very young boys, small enough to get up the chimneys. Chimney sweeps could be prone to cancer called 'sooty warts', which had no cure. Their eyes were also permanently red and runny and to harden up the cuts and grazes they received when climbing up the chimneys, they had to put up with salty water

being rubbed in. They were often forced up the hot chimneys by another boy who was positioned below them and who poked them with needles. Sometimes the chimneys were only six inches wide!

Changes to labour laws

Lots of legislation was passed to protect the children who had to work in the factories, largely between the 1840s and 1860s. The biggest change came when it was decided that it should be made illegal to employ a child under 8 years of age in a factory or workshop (1867), and that children who were aged between 8 and 13 years of age should receive 10 hours a week education as a minimum. Further important change came about in 1884 when the NSPCC was founded, and later when compulsory education came into being.

Source C

Worst Children's Jobs in History,
Taken from Charles Kingsley, 'The Water Babies'. Tony Robinson, Macmillan Children's Books, 2005

"He cried when he tried to climb the dark flues, rubbing his poor knees and elbows raw; and when the soot got into his eyes, which it did every day in the week; and when his master beat him, which he did every day in the week; and when he had not enough to eat, which happened every day in the week likewise."

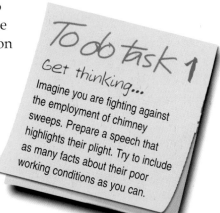

To do task 1

Get thinking...

Imagine you are fighting against the employment of chimney sweeps. Prepare a speech that highlights their plight. Try to include as many facts about their poor working conditions as you can.

Florida was sold to America by Spain in 1819.

World Link

Factory life was harsh, with long hours and many dangers. Health and safety was not the priority it is today.

- What was life like in a factory?
  - Why did some factory owners care more than others?
  - Why did people protest about the new factories?

An engraving showing a factory landscape, typical of industrial Britain.

Factory production

Textile factories were a huge part of the Industrial Revolution. They were major employers and major producers of the goods that Britain exported around the world. Wool had always been the main material used in textiles in this country, but was being replaced by cotton, which had to be imported from countries like America.

Factories could be built anywhere once steam power was available. Before this, they had to be built near to a source of water to turn the water wheels that had powered the machinery. Now, steam engines were the most efficient way to provide the constant power that was needed. The growth in these large factories meant that textile production in people's homes gradually declined. Factories also gave rise to factory towns, largely populated by the workers in the factories. Houses were small, quickly and cheaply built, and crammed together.

New technologies

Victorian engineers and scientists produced an amazing range of new and ingenious machines. Many were being introduced in the 18th-century to make factory production easier, quicker and more profitable, such as:

The spinning frame powered by water, invented by Richard Arkwright.

- Hargreaves' Spinning Jenny (1765).

- Arkwright's Water Frame (1769).

- Crompton's Mule (1779).

Source A

Worst Children's Jobs in History,
Tony Robinson, Macmillan Children's Books, 2005

"Weavers were on piece rates so the loom stopped for nothing. Armed with a brush and a sack, the young 'Scavengers' worked underneath the machine itself, scampering in and out on all fours between the metal runners, crouching low to keep out of the way of the machinery. The safety of the children depended on timing their movements with the rhythm of the Mule. If they got a hand caught in the threads of the loom or ended up in the wrong place as the heavy metal frame slid back into place, it could spell disaster."

Children at work on a loom.

Factory rules and regulations.

Although these machines improved the rate of production, people were still needed to work in the factories. Conditions in the textile factories were hard – the working days were long and tiring. Wages were nowhere near enough to make up for the huge amount of hours worked and effort put in. A 12-hour day was common. The workforce was made up of many different age groups, ranging upwards from children of seven or eight years. Men and women alike worked in the factories. The children who worked in the factories were often bought from the workhouses. Often employed as scavengers, they brushed and tidied up the pieces of stray cotton under the machines – whilst the machine was running. It could be – and was – a dangerous job. See source A.

Another job done by children was that of the piecer – simply mending the threads on the machines that had been broken.

Factory production could now take place 24 hours a day. The workers worked long shifts and had few breaks. The work and the pace could be very hard indeed. Slacking off was not acceptable and workers, especially child workers, could be beaten or, more often, fined wages.

A family affair

Whole families could be employed in the mills – men, women and children were all needed. The quality of work was judged regularly – it was very easy to lose your job if quality was not good enough, and employers used interesting methods to indicate quality. Robert Owen, a factory owner, used to attach coloured pieces of wood to the ends of machines to indicate how good the work was – white was the best and then yellow, blue and black in descending order.

RULES AND REGU

TO BE OBSERVED BY ALL

PERSONS EMPLOYED IN THIS MA.

TIME.

1.

All Persons employed in this Factory to assemble at HALF-PAST SIX O'CLOCK throughout the year.

2.

BREAKFAST TIME, HALF-PAST EIGHT to NINE.

3.

DINNER HOUR, ONE to TWO, P.M.

4.

Every day's work reckoned to terminate at SIX, P.M.

5.

All work not ready to be passed through the Warehouse by SIX O'CLOCK, P.M., on Friday, not reckoned for until the week following.

6.

Half an Hour allowed for assembling in a Morning, after which the Entrance Door will be locked; and a Quarter of an Hour at Breakfast and Dinner (except to day men.)

7.

On Saturdays, Manufacturing labour to cease at FOUR, P.M., from which time to hour for paying Wages, hands to employ themselves in cleaning rooms and benches, putting tools, &c., in order throughout the Works.

8.

Wages commence paying at FIVE O'CLOCK, P.M., on Saturdays throughout the year.

MARCH 1st, 1851.

CO

SWEARING and forbidden at all times.

During work hours SI required, and at all time conduct recommended.

SOBRIETY, CIVILITY, are indispensable for length

4.

Useful reading at proper times Publications and Prints fou TROYED, and their Owner

5.

"ON NO PRETENCE WHA ing drink, of any description, and smoking is strictly prohibit

6.

Such of the hands as take meals required to do so in their respe in the case of Girls in the room ap exclusive use.

7.

Any Person found loitering in anothe will be fined unless ve satis

Boys are not allowed to play on the Pre

CHAMBERLAIN AND CO

The Lever Brothers' factory at Port Sunlight on the Wirral.

There were some better factory owners, who believed it was their responsibilty to make sure their workers had decent living and working conditions, and earned a fair wage. Some of these factory owners built houses for their workers close to the factory. Examples include Sir Titus Salt's village at Saltaire in Yorkshire, the Lever Brother's factory at Port Sunlight on the Wirral, George Cadbury's village called Bournville, near Birmingham and Joseph Rowntree's New Earswick, near York.

Although it was definitely healthier and more enjoyable than it would have been in a 'slum', life in the towns and villages built by these **'philanthropists'** also had certain drawbacks. The factory owners might impose strict rules on the tenants and rents were often high. Workers in 'Port Sunlight', a model village built for Lever Brothers by William Lever at the end of the 19th century, had to put up with a number of these strict laws. One of the most hard-hitting rules was that the workers had to vacate their home if they lost their job.

Bourneville, near Birmingham.

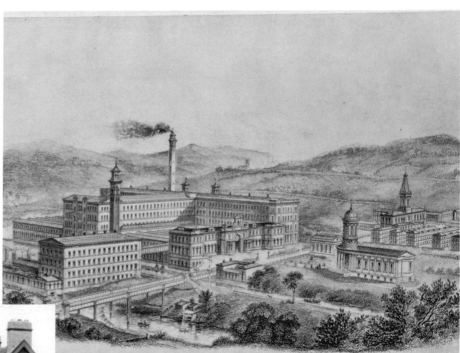

Saltaire in Yorkshire.

New Earswick, near York.

The Matchgirls

Factories, however, did not just make textiles. One factory in London, owned by a company called Bryant & May, employed women to make matches. It was an extremely dangerous job because of the chemicals involved in production, and workers often suffered a very painful condition called phossy jaw. The name was linked to the cause of the disease, which was the phosphorous that was used to make the matches 'strikeable' and flammable. Phossy jaw resulted in very painful toothache caused by an abscess in the jaw, which indicated that the bone and flesh were slowly rotting away.

The only way to solve the problem was to remove all the woman's teeth. The phosphorous that caused the problem was very toxic and the particles in the air that came off the phosphorous often settled on the food that the women ate. Unusually, these workers decided on direct action against the factory owners Bryant & May, and they held a strike, helped by campaigner Annie Besant. The Matchgirls' strike is a famous case as it direclty led to conditions within the factory improving.

 Annie Besant.

Matchgirls at work.

 **Source B** **Spartacus Educational website**

"On 23 June 1888, Annie Besant wrote an article in her newspaper, The Link. The article, entitled 'White Slavery in London', complained about the way the women at Bryant & May were being treated. The company reacted by attempting to force their workers to sign a statement that they were happy with their working conditions. When a group of women refused to sign, the organiser of the group was sacked. The response was immediate; 1400 of the women at Bryant & May went on strike."

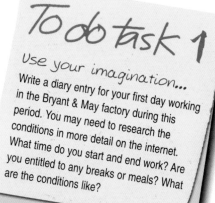

To do task 1

Use your imagination...

Write a diary entry for your first day working in the Bryant & May factory during this period. You may need to research the conditions in more detail on the internet. What time do you start and end work? Are you entitled to any breaks or meals? What are the conditions like?

Industrial protest – the Luddites

Although the factories spurred on the Industrial Revolution, some people did not like the way that machinery took over jobs previously done by men or women. These sorts of jobs had often been done at home, and been a source of income for the whole family. They were known as jobs in a 'cottage industry'. In a short period between 1811 and 1812 a group called the 'Luddites' protested against the use of mechanical weaving machines known as 'stocking frames'. Letters signed by a fictional character 'Ned Ludd' or 'General Ludd' were sent to mills in the Nottinghamshire and Leicestershire areas. The Luddites threatened to smash up these new machines, in order to protect the 'cottage industry' jobs and way of life.

Attacks were made on the mills and, in time, these attacks spread to other areas of the country such as Lancashire and Yorkshire. Workers felt they had no choice but to take direct action because, unlike today, there were no trade unions working on their behalf.

The government of the time was very concerned by the social unrest and upheaval seen in the French Revolution and was worried about the possibility of more uprisings in Britain. They took a very firm line against the Luddites so, when captured, eight of them were executed by hanging and thirteen were transported.

Transportation is where criminals were sent to America (before the American Wars of Independence) or Australia where they served their sentence. These prisoners were known as P.O.M.E (Prisoners of Mother England).

Discussion POINT ?

Would you stick up for your rights and risk losing your job?

Source C

Great Tales from English History,
Robert Lacey, Little Brown, 2006

"At one stage in 1812 there were as many as twelve thousand government troops in the four northern counties trying to hold down the rebellion of the Luddites – a significant drain on the numbers that Britain could deploy in Europe in those years in its epic struggle with Napoleon."

The Swing Riots

As more and more threshing machines were used to help increase production, a wave of violence broke out across southern and eastern England as workers smashed these machines in an attempt to save their jobs and their livelihoods. Most of these 'riots' took place in 1830 and 1831.

Rebecca Riots

Between 1839 and 1844 male protesters dressed up as women and took action against the Toll Roads that were then being built across the country. They called themselves the 'daughters of Rebecca' and smashed up and burnt down the tollgates and tollhouses. All the riots took place in South Wales.

Chartists

Source D

From the information website Wikipedia – www.wikipedia.org/wiki/chartist

Chartism was a movement for political and social reform in the United Kingdom during the mid-19th-century, between 1838 and 1848. It takes its name from the People's Charter of 1838, which stipulated the six main aims of the movement as:

Universal suffrage for all men aged 21 and older

Equal-sized electoral districts

Voting by secret ballot

An end to the need for a property qualification for Parliament

Pay for members of Parliament

Annual election of Parliament

Chartism was possibly the first mass working-class movement in the world. Its leaders have often been described as either 'physical' or 'moral-force' leaders, depending upon their attitudes to violent protest.

To do task 2

Warm up...

a) Name two ways of powering factory machines.

b) Typically, how long was a working day in a factory during the Industrial Revolution?

c) What disease did the 'Matchgirls' suffer from?

To do task 3

Get thinking...

Choose the five worst facts about working in factories during this period. Write them down and say why you think they are so bad.

To do task 4

Back to the future...

People still work in appalling conditions in factories around the world. Using the internet, find an example of such conditions, the product or products made, where it is sold and what action you think should happen, to highlight the plight of these people in your own speech or article (just like Annie Besant did).

Britain invaded the Falkland Islands in 1833.

World Link

Coal mining has been a part of British history for hundreds of years, and in this section we'll look at just why it was so important:

- Why did people work in the mines?
  - What different jobs were there in the coal mines?
  - Was coal mining a dangerous occupation?

BUZZ WORDZZ

Carbon monoxide
Deep
Drift
Hurrier
Methane gas
Ventilation

Discussion POINT ?

What was the biggest danger in the mines, and why?

Powering Britain

Coal mining was an important industry for Britain. Coal was the fuel that powered the Industrial Revolution. Although easy to use, it was quite difficult to obtain. Coal could either be 'drift' mined or 'deep' mined. Both produced very large amounts of coal, but mining was a difficult and very dangerous job. Work was hard, and the miners might not see daylight for hours on end. Whole families worked the mines – men, women and children together, each with a different job to do. They worked extremely hard to provide valuable fuel for the nation. Children who could not manage the heavy labour of hacking the coal out of the coal seam in the rock itself, could be employed down the mines doing other jobs.

 Door boys: young children, boys and girls alike, did this job. They opened and closed the **ventilation** doors within mines to allow other workers to pass by (perhaps their mother or father) and then closed the door again. These children usually worked in total darkness, so dark that you could not see your hand even if you pressed it up against your face.

 Hurriers: young children and women dragged coal carts up from the mines. A strong belt was tied to the coal cart and then around the worker's waist. The cart was then dragged out of the mine.

Dangers in the mines

Coal miners faced dangers on a daily basis. Here are just some of them:

 Choke damp: the real name for this killer was **carbon monoxide,** a toxic gas that builds up in mines and suffocates the workers. It is a silent killer, largely undetectable. Miners used to take canaries into the mine to show when 'choke damp' was present. Canaries are delicate birds and would collapse when they breathed in the carbon monoxide. This would tell the miners that it was time to leave.

Fire damp: Fire damp – **methane gas** – was a real danger for all miners. Explosive and deadly, the smallest flame was enough to ignite the gas and cause a huge explosion – a disaster. Miners used to 'explode' the gases before entering the gallery where they were working, by using a lighted candle on the end of the longest stick they could find. This problem was largely solved with the invention of the 'Davy lamp' in 1815 and when greater ventilation was put in the mines, allowing fresh air to enter.

Flooding: Water was a huge problem for the miners. Digging below the water table means that water will naturally enter the mine workings. Until the invention of powerful water pumps, miners were always at risk of drowning.

An illustration showing how a steam-powered beam engine pumped water out of the mines.

To do task 1

Use your imagination...

Imagine there has been a mining accident and you have been asked to write a report on the cause. Choose one cause and write your report on a fictional mine of your choice.

To do task 2

Back to the future...

Mining is still a big employer worldwide, with disasters still occurring. Can you find some information about a country where miners still risk their lives? Are the miners any different to the men and women who worked down the mines during the Industrial Revolution?

The Industrial Revolution saw the birth of the railways, and the invention of the steam engines that ran on them. Railways hugely expanded the growth of trade and industry across Britain, and in this section you'll find out why.

- How valuable were the navvies?
- What jobs were available on the railways once built?

Navvies

Coal mining history

Although coal mining has almost completely declined as an industry throughout Britain today, it is still possible to visit coal mines and see the conditions that the miners had to endure. One of the best is the National Coal Mining Museum in Wakefield, Yorkshire.

Navvies – or navigators – were the backbone of the labour force that built Britain's canals and railways. They were tough, hard men, famed for their fierce tempers, frequent fights and heavy drinking. Their work was dangerous and life expectancy was low. They were hired from all over the country and many came from Ireland.

Navvies being given their orders

Memorial stone laid in 1994 to commemorate the restoration of the Ribblehead Viaduct in North Yorkshire, featuring the navvies who built the structure

Source A

Fire and Steam,
Christian Wolmar, Atlantic Books, 2007

"The Navvies were an elite class of worker who could qualify for the appellation only if they fulfilled three criteria: they had to work on the hard tasks, such as tunnelling, excavating or blasting, and not on the easier types of work away from the railway: they had to live together and follow the railway, rather than merely residing at home; and they had to match the eating and drinking habits of their fellows, two pounds of beef and a gallon (8 pints) of beer a day."

Source B

Worst Children's Jobs in History, *Tony Robinson, Macmillan Children's Books, 2005*

"They wore distinctive clothes; moleskin trousers and double canvas shirts for hard wear, velveteen square-tailed coats, hobnail boots, piratical rainbow waistcoats, gaudy handkerchiefs and white felt hats off duty. They tended to be known by nicknames like 'Fighting Jack' or 'Gipsy Joe', rather than by their real names."

The navvies had a huge impact on the landscape of Britain. They laid 22,000 miles of railway track, working with only basic equipment such as a shovel and pickaxe. So dedicated were they to their jobs that they even lived where they were working, in **ramshackle** huts and shanty towns.

All the jobs on the railways were matched by jobs created in building the railways. Such was the huge demand for supplies of labour, tracks, rivets, stone, tools, explosives and other commodities, that whole new towns grew up and owe their existence solely to the railways. Such towns included Crewe, Derby and Swindon.

To do task 1
Get thinking...
Imagine you have the opportunity to meet a navvie. Write down three questions that you would like to ask the navvie.

Rail network in1850

Rail network in1890

To do task 2
Discuss...
Do you think – from the sources here – that the navvies lived a healthy life?

Navvies
Ramshackle

New transport, new jobs!

Once actually built, the railways produced many other new job opportunities: steam engines needed coal to run, so firemen were needed to shovel coal into the furnace of the engine; the engines needed drivers and mechanics. To avoid accidents, a signal man was needed who would use coloured flags or lamps to warn the drivers of danger; station masters and ticket masters were needed to sell and collect tickets; and porters were needed to carry passengers' baggage or load and unload goods – 'freight'.

Introduction

Although much of the 20th century is quite recent history, it still deserves our attention. There is a huge quantity of interesting materials available on all the decades and they could easily fill a whole book. Instead, this chapter looks at the period between the 1900 and the 1950s. Why? Well, because it was a period of great social change and will show you significant contrasts between the life experiences of various classes. Most of the topics here are covered in outline and although they may not go into great depth, it will allow you to make comparisons with the periods that came before (in the previous chapters). This will enable you to analyse what impact, if any, the major events of the First and Second World Wars had on the lives of ordinary people in Britain. When did life as we know it today became reality for the majority of people?

Who ruled ?

House of Saxe-Coburg
1901–10　　Edward VII

House of Windsor
1910–36　　George V
1936　　Edward VIII
1936–52　　George VI
1952 to today　Elizabeth II

Even in the 20th century, there were still kings and queens ruling Britain over this period.

But as we've seen before – this book isn't about kings and queens, it's about people like you!

As Britain moved into the 20th century, some historians believe it marked a distinct turning point in our history. Over this chapter you may agree, as we look at questions such as:

- Did the new century bring any major changes to the lives of ordinary people?
- How did the First World War change the lives of ordinary people?
- How easy was life at the beginning of the 20th century?

Typical working-class housing at the turn of the century

The Edwardian and second Georgian eras

Many history books believe that the Edwardian era (1901–10, with Edward VII as king) and the second Georgian era (1910–36, with George V as king), were golden times for Britain. They say this is largely because much of the population enjoyed the prosperity gained from the Industrial Revolution. Yet, they were times of much contrast between rich and poor, and an age when modern technology, on a scale that we enjoy today, had not yet arrived.

Many people lived fabulous lives alongside others who lived very hard, tough lives. More than before, the rich knew that people lived in poverty, but had very little actual experience of these conditions. The very rich – and even the emerging middle class – lived largely isolated from the poverty of the poor.

Source A — **The History of Britain and Ireland,** *Professor Kenneth O'Morgan (ed.), Oxford University Press, 1996*

"The Marchioness Curzon of Kedleston, who belonged to the very richest landowning group referred to as 'society', described how she always had a large house party for Ascot races, and all her friends had people staying with them too. There were dinner parties and balls every night during race week."

Whilst the rich enjoyed their lives of luxury, with maids, footmen and servants, ordinary working-class people had to put up with many hardships. The First World War of 1914–18 dominated the middle years of this period, but its impact will be looked at in detail in the next book in this series: *You're History! Wars and Warfare.*

Stop the Clock

The Titanic sank on 15 April 1912.

Homes, houses, towns and cities

In towns and cities, many ordinary working-class people occupied terraces, slums and tenements that were often in a very bad state of repair.

They had few facilities and amenities. As you will have seen from previous periods, many houses were still very basic and most households did not have their own toilet, at least not indoors. A night time visit to the outside toilet could be a very uncomfortable experience indeed. Running water was also a luxury that many could not enjoy, still getting it from a pump or water fountain in the street. Washing was either done in the kitchen or in the wash house, where there might have been a separate sink and tap. There were no fridges and food had to be kept in the shade, in a cold room or under a damp cloth to keep it fresh.

Some people had moved into newer semi-detached houses on the new housing estates that were being built around the country. These new houses meant improved heating, sanitation and water supplies, along with electric light fittings and sockets and a new sense of community. Householders were gradually being given the option of installing central heating systems, for the first time replacing coal fires as the main way of heating the house.

Paying the bills

One of the unforeseen problems of moving into these new houses was that you now had to pay bills for the modern technology that accompanied them. Gas, water and electricity bills all put extra pressure on the householders. This was combined with the fact that many of these new houses were rented, not owned, which meant large rent bills as well.

A contemporary advert for the very latest in Victorian technology: a central heating boiler and radiator system

To do task 1

Warm up...

a) What types of houses did working-class people typically live in?

b) Did most people have an outside or inside toliet at this time?

Discussion POINT ?

Would it always be better to move from a slum terrace into a brand-new semi-detached house?

To do task 2

Get Thinking...

In your view, what would be the worst thing about living in a terraced house at the beginning of the 20th century? Would it be the outside toilet, the lack of heating, or not having proper washing facilities? Analyse this question from a modern point of view *and* the point of view of the people who actually had to live in these conditions.

Even though this period is not very long ago, you'll find that things were very diffferent from today.

- Was there a greater variety of food available to all by the start of the 20th century?
- How did people do their shopping?
  - What standard of education was available?
  - Had health care improved by the 20th century?

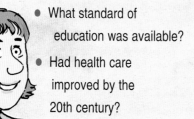

Urggh! I'm not eating that!

Food at the beginning of the century may not have been entirely to your taste. Many foods were enjoyed that most people would not consider eating today. They included offal (kidneys, liver or tripe), brawn (jellied pig's head, trotters and tail) and sheep's head, which could often be seen in the butcher's window. The working classes ate lots of this type of meat along with **dripping**, brains and ever-popular sausages. Milk was not **pasteurised** and had to be bought on the day, often coming directly to the householder from the local dairy. Many families also grew their own vegetables if they had a garden.

Shopping didn't always mean a trip down to the town. The shops often came to you. Mobile street traders sold a large selection of goods. In fact, you could get almost anything that you wanted. The 'muffin man' sold tasty muffins and crumpets and the 'winkle man' sold **winkles**. Stoves – either at home or on the street – to cook all the food on were still powered by coal.

Education

Schools had not changed much since the Victorian era. Facilities were still very basic and corporal punishment – using the cane or strap on pupils – was still the preferred method of discipline. However, pupils could now attend state schools, after the implementation of Balfour's Education Act in 1902, grammar schools, which were fee paying, or elementary schools, which were free. The school leaving age was earlier than it is today: compulsory schooling ended at the age of 14 years, when it was time to get a job. Lessons still meant writing (or copying) out on to a slate and regular visits from the 'nit nurse' had to be endured. On the plus side though, poor families could take advantage of the fact that by 1906 free school meals had become available. At lunch and break times, children entertained themselves in the playground with games such as 'conkers' and the 'whip and top'.

Fresh fish on sale from a street trader in London. This photograph was taken in 1879.

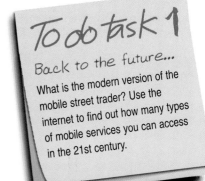

To do task 1

Back to the future...

What is the modern version of the mobile street trader? Use the internet to find out how many types of mobile services you can access in the 21st century.

Health care, hygiene, doctors and disease

Levels of hygiene, cleanliness and health were still creeping upwards but, in comparison to the standards of today, they were poor. Even basic operations might still have to be carried out at home on the kitchen table. Cleanliness in houses varied enormously and bed bugs were a common problem. For most people, the only way to get rid of these unwelcome visitors was having your bedroom smoked out with a sulphur candle.

Two great scientists

The most common disease of the period was **tuberculosis** (TB), which still affected many people. TB affects the lungs and can be spread by coughing and sneezing; it was a significant cause of death. Today, it is largely eradicated thanks to vaccination. Other illnesses that we still encounter today were common then as well and, in 1919, a massive outbreak of influenza – flu – hit Britain. However there were some advances in the field of medicine at this time, largely thanks to scientists like Marie Curie and Alexander Fleming.

Polish scientist Marie Curie was born in 1867. She won two Nobel prizes in 1903 and 1911 for her inspirational work. Together with her husband, she discovered polonium and radium and helped to develop the x-ray – a method of improving diagnosis of illness that is very much taken for granted today. The first measurement of **radioactivity** – the 'Curie' – was named after her.

Marie Curie seen in her laboratory, c 1920.

To do task 2

Warm up...

a) How did people keep food fresh without a fridge?

b) How did people get rid of 'bed bugs'?

c) Who discovered penicillin?

To do task 3

Get thinking...

Free school meals were a very important part of the changing education system in the early 20th century. What benefits would they provide for society in general? List as many as you can.

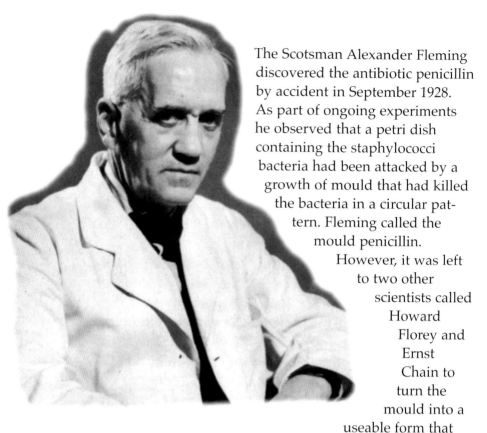

The Scotsman Alexander Fleming discovered the antibiotic penicillin by accident in September 1928. As part of ongoing experiments he observed that a petri dish containing the staphylococci bacteria had been attacked by a growth of mould that had killed the bacteria in a circular pattern. Fleming called the mould penicillin.

However, it was left to two other scientists called Howard Florey and Ernst Chain to turn the mould into a useable form that could be used by the general population, which did not happen until the era of the Second World War.

Alexander Fleming.

Stop the Clock

British Summer Tme was introduced on 17 May 1916.

To do task 4

Get creative...

Imagine you are Alexander Fleming and you want to publicise your new discovery – penicillin. Design a page for a scientific journal detailing what you have discovered and what you think its benefits to the world could be.

Source A — Advances in medicine

1910 Henry Dale unravels the mystery of shock and allergies by discovering a chemical known as 'Histamine.'

1921 Insulin is discovered by Banting and Best.

1923 Oestrogen (female hormone) is discovered by Edgar Allen.

1931 The electron microscope is invented.

1935 Testosterone (male hormone) is discovered by Ernst Laqueur.

Fancy the cinema?

While many people still enjoyed going to the music hall, cinemas showing the new 'silent movies' were becoming increasingly popular. Films were accompanied on screen by words and information about what was happening, and by music that was provided by an organist who worked in the movie theatre. By the 1930s, many films had sound – the 'talkies' – and their popularity grew even more. Stars like Laurel and Hardy, Charlie Chaplin and Buster Keaton were household names.

Professional sport had by now become extremely popular and could be watched around the country. Famous modern-day football clubs such as Manchester United were increasing in size. In fact, Manchester United was known as Newton Heath until 1902!

Other types of entertainment made popular by the Victorians were also still going strong. One good example is William Cody, (see page 85) known as Buffalo Bill.

In this first part of the 20th century entertainment was still very different to your experiences today.

- What types of entertainment did people enjoy?
- When did television become popular?

BUZZ WORDZZ

Lavish

Stan Laurel and Oliver Hardy in a scene from one of their many films.

Discussion POINT?

Do you have to be more intelligent to enjoy a silent movie?

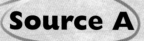 **Source A** **Lost Voices of the Edwardians,**
Max Arthur, Harper Perennial, 2007

"When Cody first came over from America he went for Kites – Cody's Kites were well known, and that was what he was exhibiting at Alexandra Palace, apart from his pistol shooting.
Captain Goudron was performing with his balloons and parachutes in the same hall."

Stop the clock

Mickey Mouse made his first appearance on 15 May 1928.

Children found their fun playing simple games with hoops and spinning tops and also enjoyed the new craze of 'soap box' racing. Richer classes enjoyed **lavish** entertainment, going to balls and dances and inviting guests into their elegant homes for dinner parties. Horse riding and hunting on country estates were very popular.

Richer women wore the latest fashions, showing off their over-sized hats covered in flowers and feathers, and they usually had long, flowing hair. Shorter hair cuts had not yet come into fashion. These women also spent many hours shopping on the fashionable Bond Street and Sloane Street in London, fast becoming the retail centre of Britain.

The rise in popularity of the cinema meant that women were exposed to new fashions, a new, more liberal way of life, make-up, new hairstyles, cigarettes and a change of attitudes towards them. Stars such as Greta Garbo, Joan Crawford and Marlene Dietrich captivated women across the globe.

A strange phenomenon known as 'television' was also making an appearance in some fortunate homes, beginning in November 1936.

DIE ELEGANTE MODE
ILLUSTRIERTE ZEITUNG FÜR MODE UND HANDARBEITEN.
№ 9 VOM 1. MAI 1900.

Studio portrait of Greta Garbo, one of the most famous female filmstars of the 20th century.

To do task 1

Warm up...

a) What new type of film was popular in this era?

b) In what year did Newton Heath become Manchester United football club?

c) On what fashionable London streets did rich women do their shopping?

To do task 2

Back to the future...

Which of the stars of silent movies are still popular and famous today? Visit some internet shopping websites to see whether any of their films are still available. Also, look through this week's TV guide, – are any silent movies still shown on television today?

To do task 3

Get creative...

Soap box racing was very popular in this period. In groups of four, design and build your own soap box racer. You may need to carry out some research on the internet to find out about the materials they were made from and what they looked like.

Money, money, money

The years between 1914 and 1918 were dominated by the First World War (or The Great War as it was known then) and many men went off to fight, whilst others worked in the war industries. While the war gave women many new opportunities in British society, immediately after it ended, times were hard for many people in Britain.

Unemployment was high but some parts of society had benefited from new social reforms. People over the age of 70 years were now able to claim a small pension following the introduction of the Old Age Pensions Act of 1908. Workers were helped by the introduction of the National Insurance Act in 1911. This guaranteed them access to free medical care and some money to live off whilst they were ill, provided that they had contributed money to the National Insurance fund from their own wages. National Insurance is still paid by workers today.

Strike and the Depression

Helpful though these were, the scale of economic problems affecting the country meant many ordinary working-class people found the 1920s tough. Conditions worsened to the point that, in May 1926, workers became so unhappy that a 'general' strike took place, where as many as two million refused to work. The main causes of the strike were issues that the coal miners had with their employers, after the government had withdrawn important subsidies that essentially kept the coal mining industry going. In sympathy to their cause, the trade unions of Great Britain asked all their members to stop working. The government's response was strong: general strikes were made illegal when the Trade Disputes Act was passed in 1927.

The Depression that affected business worldwide during the 1930s hit Britain hard, with traditional industries like coal mining declining. Many people lost their jobs. Unemployment was so high that a 'means test' was introduced that tested a family's ability to support itself, and therefore reduced the amount of support that they would receive from the government. It was based on assessing all the possible means of income that family had, including whether they could sell possessions to make ends meet.

Working patterns today are very different from in the period 1900 to 1939. Why is this the case?

- What laws made people's lives better in this period?
- What impact did the First World War have on women's employment?
- What effect did the Great Depression have on employment in Britain?

Mass protest was a feature of the General Strike. Here protesters have blocked the road, stopping the tram.

This period is also known for the hunger marches of the 1930s, which gives us an idea of just how bad the situation had become. Most marches started in Wales and the north, areas hit hardest by unemployment and poverty, and ended up in London. One of the most famous marches the 'Jarrow March'. The march took place in October 1936 and was led by an MP called 'Red' Ellen Wilkinson, accompanied by 200 workers from the shipyards in Jarrow. They were protesting about the massive shortage of jobs.

Many workers in many industries who could not support themselves lost their rental homes and ended up in doss houses, which cost a very small amount to stay in. These were better than the workhouse, that was still around, some of which had been built during the early 19th century after the 1834 Poor Law Amendment Act.

Working men on the march from Jarrow to London in 1936.

Discussion POINT?

Why were conditions in a doss house so bad?

Source A

England the Autobiography,
John Lewis-Stempel (ed.), Penguin Books, 2005

Sleeping in a doss house:

"When I got into the bed I found that it was as hard as a board, and as for the pillow, it was a mere hard cylinder like a block of wood. It was rather worse than sleeping on a table, because the bed was not six feet long, and very narrow, and the mattress was convex, so that one had to hold on to avoid falling out. The sheets stank so horribly of sweat that I could not bear them near my nose."

With unemployment rising in the traditional heavy industries like coal mining and textiles, people began to seek jobs in new 'light' industry, such as car manufacturing and assembly.

The role of women

The First World War had a huge effect on people's lives during this period. Many young men went away to fight and never came back – approximately 947,000 were killed and two million injured. The war gave women the opportunity to prove their worth in a society still dominated by men, by taking up jobs previously only performed by the men, who were away fighting.

Women were given opportunities for work they never thought they would be able to have. They did a fantastic job helping keep the war industries moving, supplying the men on the frontline. They did jobs

Gandhi's Salt March began in India on 12 March 1930.
World Link

like making munitions in the factories, driving buses and trains, and working on the land. The fact they did such a great job was one reason for women being given the partial right to vote when the war ended in 1918.

Women at work making bullets in a munitions factory in during the First World War.

Gaining the vote

Since the middle of the 19th century women had been struggling to get the vote, generating publicity and attention for their cause through groups such as the Suffragists and the Suffragettes. (This will be talked about more in Book 4 – *Rule Makers and Rule Breakers*.) The Suffragists were peaceful, relying on marches, banners and protests, whilst the Suffragettes relied on any method to make their point, including violence, chaining themselves to railings and smashing windows – as well as more radical methods.

Yet despite their obvious value during the Great War, women were discarded almost at once whenthe conflict was over. Once again their value and roles changed as the men who were returning from combat resumed their old jobs. For a brief while it seemed that the struggle for the vote which had begun with the Suffragists and Suffragettes had come to nothing. However, the Representation of the People Act was passed in 1918, giving women over the age of 30 the vote. In 1928, all women over the age of 21 years could vote.

To do task 1

Warm up...

a) In what year was the Old Age Pensions Act introduced?

b) Who was the Jarrow March led by?

c) Why did women enjoy increased job opportunities during the First World War?

To do task 2

Get researching...

Research one of the hunger marches in more detail. (Your teacher may be able to help you with this.) Produce a newspaper front page that highlights the march, the reasons why it took place and what happened during it.

To do task 3

Back to the future...

The First World War is still remembered each year on Remembrance Day (11 November). Find out what you can about how we commemorate it in the UK, and what commemorations other European countries make.

For almost all British people at the time, the 1940s were dominated by the Second World War.

- How did this war change the lives of ordinary people?
- How did the blackout affect people's lives?
- Did the war change the lives of women?

We are at war with Germany!

The Edwardian and second Georgian eras that we are studying are most famous for the war that dominated the years between 1939 and 1945. The Second World War will be looked at in detail in *You're History! Wars and Warfare*, but it had an impact on the general lives of most people and is, therefore, something we need to look at here.

Homes, houses, towns and cities

Life in the early 1940s was dominated by the war and living conditions reflected this. The British government was very worried that the civilian population would suffer huge casualties from enemy bombing attacks. To avoid showing any light and attracting enemy bombers, houses and streets had to be blacked out. The **blackout** began on 1 September 1939. All visible lights had to be blacked out at night time. This included car headlights, house lights and street signs. Even key holes had to be blocked up with putty. Householders were in charge of regulating the blackout within their own home. ARP (Air Raid Precautions) wardens patrolled the streets looking out for houses that did not follow regulations. The blackout resulted in very dark nights, and many people found this unnerving.

UNTIL YOUR EYES GET USED TO THE DARKNESS, TAKE IT EASY

LOOK OUT IN THE BLACKOUT

A government poster reminding people of the dangers of the blackout.

The blackout covered the hours from sunset to sunrise. Families made use of black fabric and paper to block the light out or even painted their windows with black paint. The people of Britain took a while to get used to these conditions, and many unnecessary accidents occurred because of the darkness. To help avoid this, the government instructed that some safety measures be put into place. These included painting the front door bell and knocker of houses with fluorescent paint and painting white lines on curbs and trees by the side of the road. Eventually, people were also allowed to carry a torch at night, provided that the beam was covered by two layers of thick tissue paper.

German aircraft did bomb British towns and cities, and provision was made for protecting civilians in air raid shelters. They could use an **Anderson shelter**, if one had been built in their garden, a **Morrisson shelter** in the house, or simply shelter under the stairs. Alternatively, public shelters had been built out of brick, with a solid concrete roof. The London Underground was even turned into a shelter and adapted to cater for the needs of the people. Brighter lights, toilets and facilities and even entertainment were made available.

Discussion POINT ?

How dark do you think it would have been during a blackout?

General housing styles had changed little, although more people were now living in semi-detached houses rather than in terraces. Significant slum areas still remained, however, especially in the major cities.

Women and war

In December 1940, after a year of war, the government realised that it would not be possible to fight the war and keep factories and industries in production whilst using only men as labour. This meant that women had to play their part in the 'war effort': doing the jobs that the men had left behind such as making munitions, planes and supplies that the frontline troops needed. They also had a key role to play in keeping the country on its feet. Fighting the war at home was called fighting the war on the 'Home Front'.

Women gradually became very proficient at a wide range of jobs such as driving buses, operating anti-aircraft guns, raising barrage balloons, driving ambulances, or delivering aircraft from factories to frontline squadrons.

BUZZ WORDZZ

Anderson shelter
Blackout
Morrisson shelter

A Balloon Site, Coventry 1943 painted by the war artist Dame Laura Knight.

'Polecats' at work.

On 7 December 1941, Japan attacked the American fleet at Pearl Harbour.

World Link

Many women joined the Women's Royal Voluntary Service (WRVS). Dressed in their green-grey tweed uniforms, red jumpers and felt hats, the WRVS did a great job serving and food, drink and mending uniforms. Women also proved themselves working the land, both in the Women's Land Army and in the **Forestry** Service. Over 80,000 women joined the Women's Land Army and women in the Forestry Service were affectionately known as 'Lumber Jills' or 'Polecats'.

Different types of work

In 1941 the National Service Act made it compulsory for women who were able to work, to fulfil their duties and play a part in the British war effort. Both married and single women had to answer the call to action, with 80% of married women and 90% of single women eventually being employed in essential war work.

In a remarkable break from tradition some women performed valuable service in ferrying combat aircraft between factories and fighter or bomber bases. These brave women flew Spitfires, Lancasters and other combat aircraft between bases to ensure that the male combat pilots had access to the planes when and where they were needed. It was by no means an easy job and women often died carrying out this vital duty. Their contribution was through the organisation called the ATA or Air Transport Auxiliary.

Some women got even closer to the front line, and served as secret agents in an organisation called the SOE – the Special Operations Executive. Some of these women who were dropped behind enemy lines were captured, interrogated and imprisoned and even put in concentration camps or prisoner of war camps.

To do task 1

Warm up...

a) On what date did the blackout begin?

b) What types of air-raid shelter were available during the Second World War?

c) What was the uniform of the Women's Royal Voluntary Service like?

To do task 2

Get thinking...

What would be the worst thing about living on the Home Front? Explain your decision and back it up with evidence.

To do task 3

Back to the future...

Research one of the more recent wars, such as the Gulf War or Afghanistan War. What precautions did the people of the areas involved have to take to avoid being bombed? Were they similar to the measures that had to be taken during the Second World War?

Source A

From the website of the *Independent* newspaper.

www.independent.co.uk/news/obituar

Pearl Cornioley spent a year in occupied France as a secret agent of Britain's Special Operations Executive (SOE). Dropped in b parachute in 1943, she worked as a courier until, after D-Day, it fell to her to organise 1,500 Resistance fighters in operations aga. the Germans.

Food

Rationing of goods, especially food, began on 8 January 1940. Everybody in the country, young and old, was issued with a ration book. This was because many goods that had been imported to Britain could no longer be obtained and other goods were simply in short supply. People began to grow their own fruit and vegetables on their own land, to add to their rations. This was called 'Digging for Victory'. They might also keep animals like chickens or pigs.

The war particularly affected people in Britain because it changed the quantity and type of food they had to eat.

- What was rationing?
- Did the war change children's education much?
- Why was the NHS created at this time?

Source A

Examples of the amounts of food allowable per person:

Butter (4oz)

Sugar (12oz)

Bacon and ham (4oz)

All per person, per week.

Source B

The War Years,
Janice Anderson, Futura, 2007

"*Rationing of basic foods was brought in gradually, starting with bacon, ham, sugar and butter in January 1940. In March, meat was rationed and in July tea, margarine, cooking fat and cheese. In March 1941, jam, marmalade, treacle and syrup were all rationed and in June the distribution of eggs was controlled, as was, in November, the distribution of milk. The last of the war time rationing came in July 1942, when sweets were put on the ration list.*"

Source C

From an original wartime information leaflet

Bacon and egg pie

2 eggs (reconstituted)

2 rashers of grilled bacon

8oz potato pastry

Salt and pepper

Method

Beat the egg. Line a plate with half the pastry. Mix the egg, potato, salt and pepper, and chopped bacon together. Pour the mixture onto the plate, cover with the rest of the pastry. Bake in a moderate oven for half an hour. Serve hot with vegetables or cold with salad.

Free! The Stork Wartime Cookery Book

There are NO FOOD PROBLEMS when you have this book!

BECAUSE some foods are rationed there's no need to go short of nourishment or to put up with dull and uninteresting meals. With the help of Stork and the new Stork Wartime Cookery Book you will find that meals are not only just as attractive as they were before, but just as nourishing. And as for cooking Stork for spreading as well your full supply of the essential Sunshine Vitamins A and D. Get your copy of The Stork Wartime Cookery Book right away! Remember — it's FREE!

STORK MARGARINE
Wins your favour with its flavour

Cut this out and post today

BUZZ WORDZZ

Evacuate
Population density

Education

Schooling was largely interrupted by the war and evacuation. When the threat of a German invasion loomed large over Britain, a decision was made to evacuate children and 'priority women' (women with children under school age and pregnant women) away from the cities that would be the targets for enemy bombing. Sometimes whole schools were evacuated, including the teachers. Evacuation was not a compulsory scheme, it was voluntary. You volunteered for your children to be evacuated and people volunteered to take your children in. The children continued to have a normal school education in the place where they had been evacuated to. Many of the children who were evacuated came from areas with a high population density and were largely working class. Children didn't have to be evacuated through the official government scheme; arrangements could also be made to stay with family relatives who lived in quieter, countryside areas.

Around 1.5 million people were evacuated at the start of the war.

 Evacuated children line up to be sorted. The first wave of evacuations in September 1939 saw 1.5 million people relocated.

Source D

Wartime Britain 1939–45,
Juliet Gardiner, Headline, 2004

"Children took a handbook or case containing the child's gas mask, a change of underclothing, night clothes, house shoes, or plimsolls, spare stockings or socks, a toothbrush, a comb, towel, soap and face cloth, handkerchiefs: and if possible a warm coat or mackintosh."

Health and health care

This decade saw the introduction of the National Health Service (NHS) in 1948, two years after the initial NHS Act of 1946. The Minister of Health, Aneurin Bevan, was the creator of the NHS. This was the first time that free medical treatment was available for anybody who needed it, rather than just those who could afford it. It built on the improved health of the nation caused by rationing, which had encouraged people to have a more balanced diet. Penicillin was also becoming more widely available and had been used on the injured troops on the battlefields.

In its quest to bring all essential medical services together in one place, the NHS really was an amazing system. Rather than just fight diseases it aimed to prevent them as well. However, it was not expected that it would be placed under quite as much strain as it is today. Its goal of providing medical care to everybody, for free, was perhaps ambitious as the current NHS struggles to maintain that provision of free healthcare for all in the face of ever-rising costs.

To do task 1

Warm up...

a) When did rationing of food begin?

b) What was 'Digging for Victory'?

c) When was the National Health Service introduced?

To do task 2

Get thinking...

How would your life change today if you had to observe a blackout? Would you be able to cope? Using a minimum of 50 words, outline ten things that you would find hard and then explain which one would be the most difficult to cope with.

To do task 3

Back to the future...

Have any of the modern wars (the two Gulf Wars for instance or the war in Afghanistan) forced citizens to observe a blackout? Why do you think this is the case? This task may require some research so the internet may be useful.

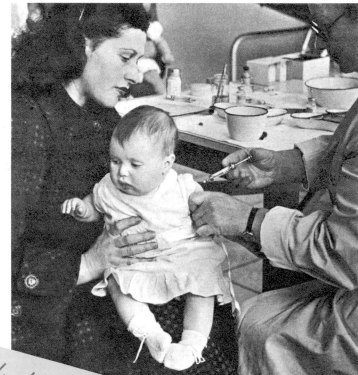

A small child being vaccinated against diptheria.

By 1945 Britain had fought in two world wars in a little over 30 years. After so much upheaval to everyday life, you might expect that Britain would change enormously.

- How soon did people get back to normal after the Second World War?
- Was everyday life becoming more like we know it today?

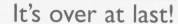

It's over at last!

The end of the Second World War in 1945 meant the beginning of a new era for Britain. 6.5% of all the houses in Britain had been destroyed by enemy bombing during the war. Many of the houses that remained still had tin baths that had to be filled up in front of the fire, and an outside toilet! It was time for change.

Many houses had been destroyed or damaged during the war and these needed replacing. In 1945, the government decided that instead of building lots of new houses, **prefabricated** buildings were to be used in large numbers. New house building was a priority for the government, especially with the 'Baby Boom' spurred on by the servicemen returning home from war. Their initial aim was to build 4,000,000 new homes in the first decade after the war ended. At this time many families could only dream of central heating, and modern appliances that we may take for granted today were equally unobtainable.

'Prefabs'

The factories that had turned out aircraft, tanks and guns in the war, now turned to building prefabricated houses, planned to have just a ten-year lifespan – a form of temporary housing. Some have survived so long now that they are being recorded as listed buildings. These new houses were equipped with fitted kitchens including gas cookers and fridges.

Many of these new houses were also built on new housing estates, and there was a slow change from people renting accommodation to buying their own home. DIY became a new hobby amongst these new householders, who strived to make these homes their own. The government even went as far as building new towns, such as Runcorn in Cheshire, or rebuilding old ones, such as Stevenage in Hertfordshire. People who had been bombed out of their houses during the Second World War now had the option to buy one of the new prefabricated houses. These were very modern, made from a metal frame and covered in materials such as asbestos, aluminium, hardboard and concrete. The population soon called them 'palaces for the people'.

Keeping clean

As most people did not have the luxury of washing machines, the

Source A The memory store

> *"Two massive technological advances improved modern domestic (home) life – 19th century sewage systems that allowed cities to grow without the risk of disease, and early 20th century electric power that made household machinery and lighting possible."*

Listed building
Prefabricated
Temporary

weekly wash was still done at home in the scullery with a washboard and a mangle. Clothes were rubbed against the washboard and the water was squeezed out with the mangle. The clothes were then pegged on the clothes line. For many households, Friday night was bath night – although any night would have done equally as well – and the tin bath was placed in front of the fire and filled with hot water from the kettle. Many houses still had open fires, usually requiring coal or wood, so houses had a coal cellar or a cupboard under the stairs where the coal was stored. Things were improving though, with vacuum cleaners, washing machines and steam irons becoming available to most by the end of the decade.

National Service

Despite changes in many areas one thing did not disappear: National Service. Although in decline, the British Empire still needed a strong, armed Britain as a world power. So thousands of young men, despite the end of the Second World War, still had to do their duty. In fact National Service was not stopped until 1960. Men had to serve 18 months in the forces and then stay on the reserve list for a further four years, so great was the threat of further conflict around the world.

Discussion POINT?

How clean do you think houses would have been before all the new domestic technology became available?

To do task 2

Get thinking...

Which items of domestic technology could you cope without? Which items could you never imagine giving up? Write a paragraph explaining your decisions and why.

Source B
From the website of the National Army Museum

The government initially imposed an 18-month period of service on conscripts, but this was later extended to two years with three and a half on the Reserve. By 1951 around 50% of the Army's strength consisted of National Servicemen. They came from all walks of life and from all social backgrounds. National Servicemen served in the scorching deserts of Palestine and Aden, the humid jungles of Malaya and the icy hills of Korea.

A total of 395 National Servicemen were killed on active service in these areas. Many conscripts considered their service as the best years of their lives and gained new friendships, new skills and the experience of foreign travel. Others saw it as a dreadful experience to be reluctantly endured at best.

More and more parts of everday life for British people changed as the 1940s became the 1950s.

- How did food, education and hygiene improve?
- What was the school curriculum like in the 1950s?

Food and shopping

This was still a time when shopping as we know it today, at supermarkets or specialist high-street shops, was unheard of. Numerous traders went from door to door selling a range of things. These were many and varied, from the pop man who sold fizzy drinks such as Dandelion and Burdock, to the coal man who sold the coal for the fires. A regular sight, and one that still exists today, was the milkman. Another, less common sight today, was the rag and bone man.

Rationing of certain foods was still in force, and in fact did not end until 1954. Diet, however, was improving. Much more meat was now available, although fruit was still not widespread again until trade with foreign countries became re-established.

Education

Schools were changing. Pupils now had to take an 11 Plus examination, which decided whether they went to a grammar school, secondary modern, or comprehensive (although comprehensive schools did not really become popular until the 1960s). At secondary modern schools boys learned skills like woodwork and metalwork, and girls learned skills centred around the household.

Health and health care

The general health of the population was not as good as it is today, with poliomyelitis being a big killer, along with other well-known illnesses like whooping cough and flu. Polio could cause paralysis as it causes an inflammation of the spinal chord. Today, it has been eradicated thanks to vaccination.

The rag and bone man got his name from collecting rags – to be turned into paper or fabric – and bones, to be turned into glue.

A class in a 1950s schools being taught about electricity and wiring a plug.

Source A

The 50s and 60s, The Best of Times,
Allison Pressley,
Michael O'Mara, 2003

"The rag and bone man shouted 'Any old rags and bones', which sounded like 'ennyoleraanbo'."

Source B

The 50s and 60s, The Best of Times,
Allison Pressley, Michael O'Mara, 2003

"I had eczema as a child, which got infected and turned into impetigo, so I ended up with huge thick scabs all over my face. I had to go to an isolation ward where they treated me by putting a thick mix of starch all over my face every night, covered with a tubular bandage with holes for my eyes. When I woke up in the morning the whole thing had set rigid. Then the nurses would come around with a trolley, with a huge bowl of calamine lotion. They would come into the room and grab hold of the bottom of this cast over my face and pull the whole thing off. With it would come all the scabs."

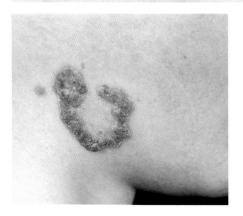

Impetigo was another common complaint from the time: it is an extremely infectious disease that is a form of **eczema** and can be easily spread through touch. The skin irritation is often like a crusty red blister and can 'weep' as the infection progresses. Again, medical advances over this period mean it is now easily cured.

BUZZ WORDZZ

Eczema
Impetigo
Traders

To do task 1

Use your imagination...

Read source B about being in hospital in the 1950s. Extend the story and add more detail. To do this, imagine that you are the patient. You can add a beginning and an end to the story.

Source C

The 50s and 60s, The Best of Times,
Allison Pressley, Michael O'Mara, 2003

"Even going to the loo was traumatic, using toilet roll called 'Izal Germicide' which felt like you were using tracing paper."

On 7 October 1959, the far side of the moon was seen for the first time.

To do task 2

Back to the future...

a) Find out which vaccinations are compulsory for all children, at what age you are given them, and how much they cost per vaccination.

b) Why do you think that the government is so keen for people to be vaccinated?

By now you might think that entertainment must have been close to what we take for granted today. Or was it?

- What was the holiday camp and why was it so popular?
- What was television like in the 1950s?

Hi de hi!

Blackpool Beach in the 1950s. The tradition of taking a ride on a donkey was started by the Victorians.

Rebuilding family life after the war was essential and families made the most of their new leisure time.

The re-opening of the beaches after the wartime anti-tank devices and mines had been removed meant that people could once again go to the seaside. Trips to the seaside were very popular and families made the most of the opportunity to have a good time whatever the weather! People tucked into fish and chips and cockles whilst writing postcards designed by the famous artist Donald McGill to their friends back home. Watching the Punch and Judy man, walking along the promenade and onto the pier, going on boat trips and eating ice-cream were the ingredients of a good holiday.

Holiday camps were becoming an increasingly popular holiday choice. Although, to you today, it may seem that life within the camps was strictly controlled and the timings of activities and meal times were strict, many families loved their atmosphere. They were the first **package holidays**, with everything included in the price. Holiday camps like Butlins had games and activities led by entertainment staff, the easily-recognisable 'Red Coats'. They were much like a mini-community and everybody could find something to interest them.

BUTLIN'S HOLIDAY CAMP
IT'S QUICKER BY RAIL

Source A

Fifties Britain,

Nigel Perryman, Francis Frith Collection, 2002

"At Butlin's Filey camp, for example, you could learn to master a bicycle built for rather more than two, to the unconcealed admiration of the onlookers. Or you could have a go at roller-skating, while crowds watched to see if you fell over. Fairgrounds and boating lakes were always popular, while the swimming pool was often the focus of a camp's activities. Some camps even sported miniature railways, chair lifts, water rides and memorials."

BUZZ WORDZZ

Coronation
Package holidays

Those with slightly more money could also go abroad, with the first foreign package holidays available.

More things to do...

Another way of getting away from it all was in a caravan and more families were making use of this mobile holiday home. Zoos were opening across the country and families could also enjoy a day at the races, or at a fairground on the dodgems and the helter-skelter. The Lake District and the Peak District were made National Parks in 1951 and many people flocked to these open spaces.

Young children did not have the entertainment options of today: their choices were much more basic. Boys played with train sets, pedal cars, model aeroplanes and Airfix model sets. Girls played with dolls and enjoyed games like skipping, rounders or roller-skating. Other board games like 'Ludo' and 'Tiddlywinks' were also popular. Adults played card games and went to clubs and societies like the Round Table, or maybe the occasional fancy dress party.

Holidays Abroad by AIR

1951

THOS. COOK & SON LTD.
DEAN & DAWSON LTD.

Huge street celebrations also occurred occasionally, especially for events like the Festival of Britain in 1951 and the **Coronation** of Queen Elizabeth II in 1953.

Stop the Clock

Blackpool's illuminations were first switched on in 1879.

The growth of television

Television became increasingly popular in the 1950s, with new programmes and more affordable television sets. 1953 saw the launch of ITV, giving viewers a choice of two channels to watch! More families had their own television and could enjoy these new programmes. As television became more popular, children's programmes like *Watch with Mother*, *Andy Pandy* and *Muffin the Mule* were big favourites as was sci-fi hit *Lost in Space*.

Not everyone could afford the luxury of a television set. For some, the radio was still an important source of entertainment and many families gathered around the set and enjoyed programmes like *Listen with Mother*. Television shows that captivated audiences in the 1950s included *Bill and Ben*, the *Quatermass Experiment, Rag, Tag and Bobtail, Crackerjack*, the *Eurovision Song Contest* and *Benny Hill*.

A television set from the 1950s.

On 6 May 1954, Roger Bannister ran the first four-minute mile.

World Link

To do task 1

Back to the future...

Holiday camps still exist today. Research one on the internet. Has the entertainment or quality of service changed? Are they still as popular as ever?

To do task 2

Get creative...

Find out about one of the games from the 1950s that still exists today. Is it still as enjoyable to play, even with the internet, mobile phone and video game technology around today?

To do task 3

Challenge...

This is the end of the ride through the ages and over the years. Complete your analysis of the changing face of ordinary people's lives by writing an extended piece of writing on how people's lives have changed over the last 1000 years. If you are able to do this well, you really are getting good at history!

Discussion POINT ?

Could you cope without television?

You probably take road travel for granted, but people have not always been able to move around as quickly and easily as we can now. This topic looks at:

- Which criminals posed a problem for early road users?
- Were highway robbers really 'gentlemen'?
- What has been the biggest development in road travel?

Don't walk, it's quicker to drive!

We are all very good at taking our transport for granted, so much so that the government is always trying to get us to walk, use public transport, or share our cars. If you think about how much you rely on a car, or a bus, it may come as a shock to you. Imagine how many calories you would burn if you walked all the time!

Cars are a relatively new invention, as you will discover, so how did people get about before the car arrived?

Tudor travel

In the Tudor period most people walked to their destination, or used a horse or mule to carry the goods that they were transporting. Some rode horses, although they were a relatively expensive form of transport and could be easily stolen. Horse-drawn coaches became more common over time, but it cost a lot of money to have a seat on one. Roads actually became busy, dangerous places because of the growing numbers of people and carriages on them, and there are numerous accounts of people being killed by horse-drawn carriages. Not every journey required a horse though, so how did people get about when the journey was shorter?

Sedan chairs

The answer is that people could hire a taxi, well sort of! Sedan chairs were the Tudor and Stuart version of the taxi. They were essentially a wooden box on two poles, carried by two people with extra support of the weight on the poles with leather shoulder straps. The sedan chairs could be rented by individuals, who could flag them down like a modern taxi. The carriers (or drivers) would go as far as you wanted, and the cost was up to you to bargain. If you ran out of money you could simply jump out!

An early Sedan chair.

To do task 1

List all the types of transport available to us today. Then rate the different types in order of usage and importance.

Discussion POINT?

What would your life be like if you had to walk everywhere? Are there any parts of your life that wouldn't be changed?

Isn't this road awful?

The energy of a sedan chair bearer only lasted so long, which meant that if you wanted to go a long way, you had to risk the dangers of the roads yourself. But the truth is that you would probably have been quicker walking. Many roads in this period were very poorly maintained. Roads that were well maintained were usually being kept in good order (or not as the case may have been when money ran short) by the local parish. Only with the introduction of **turnpike trusts** in the mid-17th century and toll roads, bringing over 15 000 miles of higher quality roads to Britain, did road travel become easier.

Better roads

The surface of the roads also improved hugely when two engineers, Thomas Loudon McAdam and Thomas Telford, came up with a new process for building road surfaces, one of which was known as macadamising.

This contemporary painting shows the Kensington Turnpike with the toll house and gates visible on the right.

Macadamising is a system that relies on crushed stones and gravel being placed on a bed of larger stones. Inbuilt into the road is a camber or curve that allows the water to drain off the road. The addition of tar to bind it all together results in "Tar-macadam" which is seen on modern roads.

This at last allowed high-speed coaches to make fast journeys between cities. The record time for a journey from London to Edinburgh in 1830 was 42 hours and 33 minutes, still very slow by the standards of today.

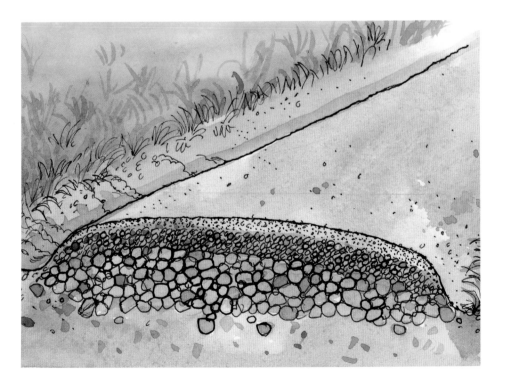

Discussion POINT

Why do we need to get around?

Why do we need transport?

Highway robbery

So the better roads made everything better, or did they? Other problems began to appear that made the bumps and potholes seem very tame in comparison. A bigger danger was the ruthless highwaymen who roamed the roads, robbing unsuspecting people of their valuables.

Here are just a few of Britain's most famous highwaymen. Imagine meeting them on a dark night!

- **John 'Swift Nick' Nevison:** born in Sheffield in 1639, Nevison was the son of a wool merchant. He had previously had a career as a soldier and was easily recognisable as he was tall and slim. His fame is based around a long ride he made from Kent to York, travelled in a day. He was in reality a notorious murderer who was hung at York Castle on 4 May 1684.

- **Dick Turpin:** born in 1706 in Essex, Turpin was the son of a farmer. His early career was that of a butcher and a cattle thief. He also had a brief stint as a smuggler and was a key member of the Gregory Gang. Dick Turpin had a nasty habit of holding his victims over an open fire, torturing them. He was so notorious that a £50 reward was offered for his capture. To avoid this, he took on the name of John Palmer, but in 1739, the law did catch up with him, and he faced the gallows on 19 April.

- **James Maclaine** and **William Plunkett:** proving that history is far from dead or relegated to the past, these two gentlemen highway robbers were the subject of a recent film. Maclaine was the son of a **Presbyterian** minister and Plunkett was an apothecary who had faced financial ruin. Whilst Maclaine was hung on 3 October 1750, his partner Plunkett was never brought to justice.

Dick Turpin has his fate foretold by a gypsy woman as he passes by a gibbet.

Lord Eglington is robbed by Maclaine.

The Victorians

Road transport was very slow developing, with little progress made over a long period of time. Even by the Victorian era transport was still mostly horse-drawn, even fire engines were pulled by horses. Roads within the cities and towns were often very dirty, muddy and covered in horse manure. A crossing sweeper brushed a clean path for pedestrians to walk over. Buses too were pulled by horses and the famous Shillibeer's Omnibus had begun its journeys in July 1829. If you didn't want to use a bus, you could still use a stagecoach.

Source A — The Bus We Loved, Travis Elborough, Granta Books, 2005

"*Hackney coachmen possessed a complete monopoly in the busy central districts. Congestion was a fear – even then – and stagecoaches, including those journeying short distances across the city, could pick up or set down passengers only at designated points, usually inns.*"

Bishop's Road, Fulham, London circa 1870 – 1900.

Powered road machines were beginning to make an appearance but were viewed with some doubt. The **Locomotive** Act of 1865 had laid down rules regarding the movement of 'powered' machines on the roads (usually steam driven ones). This act gained the name 'The Red Flag Act' because a man was expected to walk in front of the vehicle waving a red flag. The speed limit of such vehicles was set at 2 mph in a town and 4 mph in the countryside.

Gradually, motorised road travel was becoming more popular, although in 1905 there were only 20 motorbuses on the road compared to 1400 horse buses. However, by the end of 1905 the number of motor buses had grown to 230.

To do task 3

Imagine that you are the person who is describing the first sighting of the motorbus in Source B. In another 100 words, carry on the story describing what you saw and what you felt at the time.

Source B

Lost Voices of the Edwardians,
Max Arthur, Granta Books, 2005

"I remember seeing the first motorbus. It must have been in about 1907. Somebody shouted, 'Quick! Quick! Come and look! There's a bus without a horse!' It was a very primitive thing running along in Islington, making an awful lot of stink and noise, but everybody stood up to look."

The first self-propelled bus in London, 1902.

A London general type 'b' bus, 1910.

A bus is now a form of transport that is truly taken for granted and the famous Routemaster bus, first seen on 24 September 1954, is still a classic symbol of British transport. Buses are used all the time now, and some of you may use them everyday - and yet, they weren't even motorised as recently as 100 years ago. Things have really moved quickly.

Fancy a new car?

Today buses are by far outnumbered by cars, but it has only been relatively recently that the car became a common sight on our roads. Until the 1920s a car was something that many people could simply not afford. It was only the period between the two World Wars that saw many people purchasing their first motor vehicles. Gottlieb Daimler and Karl Benz had produced the first car in 1886 and the first mass-produced car was the 'Model T Ford', first sold in 1908.

Between 1908 and 1927, 15,000,000 cars were sold worldwide. From the 1950s onward the car had truly captured the public's imagination and by the 1960s car production was a major UK industry, with numerous car factories churning out cars daily. Many people had taken to the roads and, to cater for the increased demand, Britains first Motorway – the M1 – was opened in 1959.

The world's first "motor carriage" was produced by the German company Daimler Benz.

M1 Motorway, 1959.

A map showing the coverage of the M1 from 1950 to the present day.

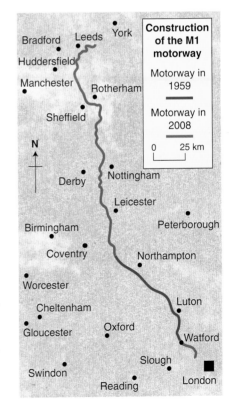

135

Dad, what car did you drive?

Many young people in the 1960s and 1970s loved their first cars, being able to choose from numerous exciting models. Source C lists just a few. Why don't you ask your mum or dad about them?

Source C My Dad Had One of Those,
Giles Chapman and Richard Porter, BBC Books, 2007

Ford Escort, Morris Marina, Austin 1100, Hillman Avenger, Vauxhall Viva, Austin Allegro, Hillman Hunter, Triumph 2000, Ford Zephyr, Mini Clubman, Hillman Imp, Ford Anglia, Jaguar XJ6, Triumph Dolomite, Ford Popular, Rover P4, Citroën 2CV, Reliant Robin, Opel Manta, Ford Capri, Triumph Stag, Volvo 245, Citroën GS and Ford Cortina.

Source D

My Dad Had One of Those,

Giles Chapman and Richard Porter, BBC Books, 2007

"*Otherwise known as the Harry Potter Car, in its day the Ford Anglia was slightly less magical, being an honest and unsophisticated little car for Dads anywhere. The designers went nuts with their copy of the Big Book of American Cars, shamelessly nicking all the flashy bits from the 1950s US land yachts and shrinking them to a size that would actually fit into Britain.*"

Today car production is a multi-billion pound world business, and the vehicles themselves are a world away from the first models that hit our streets little more than 100 years ago. Who would have thought that you can now travel around in cars that can cost as much as somebody's house, or more in certain cases. As well as still being a functional form of transport, some cars are now, in some people's eyes, little more than expensive toys.

Lamborghini, Porsche and Mercedes are some of the motor manufacturers whose cars are most often bought by the rich or famous, and in some cases the actual car's appeal might have little to do with practicality, and more to do with making a statement about the owner. One such example is the Bugatti Veyron supercar with a top speed of 252 mph and an 8 litre W16 engine. When launched its price was a cool € 1 million. But where is the practicality in producing such a car? Who actually needs a vehicle that goes that fast? Surely nobody does, but that has not stopped it becoming one of the world's most desirable cars.

▲ The Bugatti Veyron

Discussion POINT ?

Why do people today love their cars?

BUZZ WORDZZ

Locomotive
Presbyterian
Turnpike trusts

To do task 5

Get researching...

Research one of the cars from the 1960s and 1970s. What were they like and what could you expect to find in the interior?

You may wish to ask a member of your family to help you.

Present your findings to the class, perhaps comparing your chosen car to a modern car.

To do task 4

Warm up...

a) What is a sedan chair?

b) Name two highway robbers.

c) What did the Locomotive Act do?

d) Name two engineers who improved road surfaces.

e) What was the first mass-produced car?

f) Name two cars from the 1960s and 1970s.

The Suez Canal was opened in 1869.

World Link

Rail travel revolutionised transport in Britain, so it's an important part of the overall travel topic:

- How long have people been able to travel by rail?
- How fast were the steam locomotives?
- Did the London Underground have an impact on travel worldwide?

Richard Trevithick, railway engineer, 1816.

All aboard!

Train travel is usually quick and easy and increasingly much more so than road travel. Probably only a few of you use the train on a regular basis though. Trains developed much earlier than cars, and they are a more ecologically-friendly form of transport if they are powered by electricity, so why not use them?

Richard Trevithick, a Cornishman, built the first road-going vehicle powered by anything other than horses in 1800, but it crashed into a ditch and the following explosion meant the end of the experiment. He also developed the first ever steam locomotive in 1804, although it was not until George Stephenson (1781–1848) took the basic idea and improved it in his 'Rocket' engine, that travel by steam locomotive became viable. The first passenger service was the Swansea to Mumbles railway and the first railway was the Stockton to Darlington railway.

We need a competition!

Steam locomotives, as they were called, were a new phenomenon. The word locomotive literally means 'moving to or from a place' and they could not only transport goods, they could also move passengers.

Many different companies tried to make their fortune from the railways, but many failed. One that suceeded was the Liverpool to Manchester Railway, who celebrated the opening of their new route by organising a competition to see who could produce a locomotive engine that could be reliably used to transport people and goods. The competition was known as the Rainhill Trials and took place on 15 September 1830 and thousands of spectators lined the tracks to watch.

The engines had to weigh a maximum of 4.5 tonnes, have a maximum boiler pressure of 50 pounds per square inch, cost a maximum of £500 and pull 20 tonnes at 10mph. The trains that were scheduled to compete were the Cycloped, Novelty, Perseverance, Sans Pareil and the Rocket. The winner of the competition was the Rocket designed and built by George and Robert Stephenson, which reached the terrific speed of 29 mph.

However, the excitement of the competition was marred by a horrible accident. A local MP, Mr Huskisson, was crushed by the Rocket. (see Source C)

Source A

Fire and Steam,
Christian Wolmar,
Atlantic Books, 2007

"It was actually the Stockton to three collieries near Bishop Auckland line via Darlington."

Source B

Great Tales from English History,
Robert Lacey, Little Brown, 2006

"With steam oozing from her twin pistons, angled on either side of her boiler like the haunches of some gigantic frog ready to leap forward along the track, the Rocket embodied all the power and menace that frightened people about the railways: birds would be killed by the smoke warned the doom mongers, and cows' milk would curdle as the noisy trains sped past; it was even suggested that passengers' lungs would collapse under the pressure of high speeds. On the other side of the Pennines, the Duke of Cleveland had held up the Stockton and Darlington line for three years for fear of what it would do to his foxes."

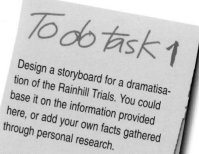

To do task 1

Design a storyboard for a dramatisation of the Rainhill Trials. You could base it on the information provided here, or add your own facts gathered through personal research.

◀ An illustration of the Rocket thundering past.

Source C

Fire and Steam,
Christian Wolmar,
Atlantic Books, 2007

"The Times *refers to the wheel going over his left thigh and squeezing it almost to jelly.*"

The ROCKET of Mr. Robt. Stephenson of Newcastle
Which drawing a load equivalent to three times its weight travelled at the rate of 12½ miles an hour, & with a carriage & passengers at the rate of 24 miles. Cost per mile for fuel about three-halfpence.

◀ The Rocket as it took part in the Liverpool and Manchester Railway competition, which it won.

139

To do task 2

You were a passenger on the station at Wigan on the fateful day in 1873, and were there when the Euston to Scotland train derailed. Describe what you saw and felt.

Source E

The New York Times,
September 1873

For the last five or six weeks – ever since the Wigan disaster, in fact – there has been scarcely a day without an accident of some kind. August is a very busy tourist month…trains are overcrowded, there are delays at the stations, and engine-drivers have to make up by extra speed for the time which is lost…and there is less caution than usual at a season when caution should be increased. The rush of accidents follows as a matter of course.

Come on, let's go on a train!

As the railways became more popular, many passengers made their first journey on a train with a sense of excitement.

Source D

England the Autobiography, *John Lewis-Stempel (ed.), Penguin Books, 2006*

"You cannot conceive what the sensation of cutting the air was; the motion is as smooth as possible too. I could either have read or written; and as it was, I stood up, and with my bonnet off, drank the air before me. The wind, which was strong, or perhaps the force of our thrusting against it, absolutely weighed my eyelids down."

Don't worry, it's safe!

Accidents, unfortunately, were common on the early railways. On 2 August 1873 at 1:20am, the regular service from Euston to Scotland was travelling through Wigan station in Lancashire, when sparks became visible from the back of the train. Some of the carriages had become derailed and as the trained hurtled through the station creating a deafening noise, the loose carriages crashed and smashed against the station platform, with more and more carriages breaking free from the main train. Thirteen passengers were killed and 30 were injured. Despite all this, the train was back on its way to Scotland just 90 minutes later.

The need for speed

Human beings have a natural desire to constantly challenge and improve most aspects of their lives, and being obsessed with speed soon decided that the trains should be going faster. Railway companies tried therefore to develop faster trains. Steam trains actually reached top speeds close to those that the modern trains can reach. One good example of a fast train is The Flying Scotsman.

The Flying Scotsman

The Flying Scotsman is a famous locomotive, but the name 'Flying Scotsman' was actually the name of a regular train service, which ran at 10:00am every day from London King's Cross to Edinburgh. For the Empire exhibition of 1924, the LNER (London and North East Railway) converted engine number 1472 into The Flying Scotsman, complete with name plate. It was painted in apple-green paint and exhibited, looking splendid. People marvelled at it.

To draw more publicity for LNER and the London to Scotland service, the engine was to be involved in a time trial. On 1 May 1928, driver Albert Pilsworth at the controls, The Flying Scotsman departed from King's Cross. It travelled the 392 miles non-stop to Edinburgh, clocking up a terrific 90 mph along the way. This was the beginning of a long period of service for the engine and it was only retired from regular service in 1963.

The Mallard

The Flying Scotsman, however, was not the fastest steam train ever developed. This title went to the Mallard, nicknamed the 'Blue Streak'. It is still the fastest steam train ever built, reaching the impressive speed of 126mph on 3 July 1938.

The Mallard was owned by the same company who owned The Flying Scotsman, the LNER Railway Company, and can now be seen in the National Railway Museum in York.

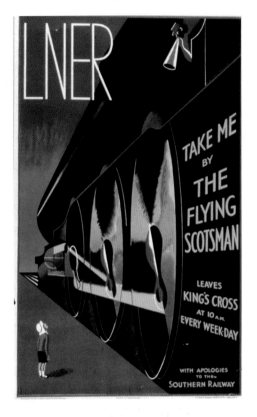

A railway poster advertising The Flying Scotsman.

The Mallard, nicknamed 'Blue Streak' – the fastest steam train reaching 126 mph in 1938.

To do task 2

York Railway Museum is home to a number of historic trains. Visit their website and then make a short presentation – perhaps using Powerpoint – about what you could see during a visit to the museum.

141

Discussion POINT **?**

Why did trainspotting become a hobby?

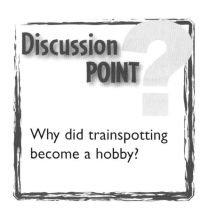

Source F

Mallard: How the World Steam Speed Record was Broken,
Don Hale, Aurum, 2005

"It was only after the train had reached King's Cross that the dynamometer car records could be examined and the record speed confirmed. A preliminary examination of the record showed that 124.5 mph had been reached for 10 seconds and later that 125 mph had been attained for 5 seconds. Some time later 126 mph was finally established, only for 1 second, or about 60 yards."

Going underground

Train travel above ground is fine when there is sufficient space to lay the tracks. In crowded cities this is not possible, therefore an alternative is needed. This alternative came in the form of the first underground railway system.

A map of the London Underground system – This is a very special sot of map; can you find out why? Here's a clue – try the Geography department in your school!

London Transport special Coronation map 1952.

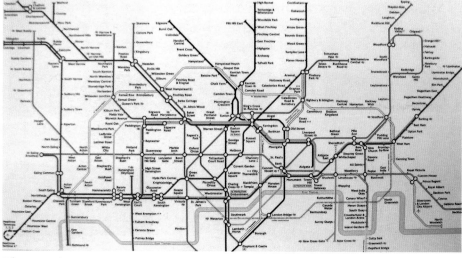

The London Underground system was built by the Victorians, buried between 30 to 250 feet below the ground. It is a fantastic, wonderful feat of engineering. It was a vast project that required huge amounts of manpower and a terrifically gifted engineer to make it happen. Sir John Fowler, an engineer from Sheffield, led the project and called upon workers from all over the country. It cost a huge amount of money to build, relying on many generous investors. The building of the system was a feat beyond belief, requiring the demolition of many houses and buildings and numerous pipes, drains and sewers had to be moved to make way for it.

The navvies all risked their lives to ensure that the project was a success. Not only was it a great drain on both money and manpower, it also demanded that a number of bills be pushed through parliament, usually one for each new line or track. It was a difficult project to manage mainly because of its size and complexity. Work had to be split between two separate shifts, continuing throughout the whole day. Building the London Underground required a huge program of slum clearances, and great care had to be taken not to weaken the foundations of any buildings that the lines ran underneath.

Sir John Fowler, civil engineer, 1882.

To do task 4

Get researching...

Find out about the other major underground railway systems in the world today.

What can you discover about their history?

Do any similarities exist between them and the London Underground?

The construction of the underground, 1957.

THE ROOF OF LONDON
HAMPSTEAD
TRAVEL BY LONDON'S UNDERGROUND

The whole idea of a railway under the city was a very large gamble and many people simply did not believe that it would ever work. Parliament took a long time to agree to the whole project. The engineering aspect was equally adventurous because building tunnels underneath houses had never before been completed and many houses were actually damaged, leading to claims for compensation. (See Source G)

Many people thought that a train in a tunnel would suffocate the passengers, but on opening day on 9 January 1863 the anticipation was great.

A poster advertising travelling to Hampstead by underground.

Source G

The Subterranean Railway,

Christian Wolmar,
Atlantic Books, 2004

"The Landlord of the Rising Sun in the New Rd claimed £1,100 arguing that cracks had appeared in his wall, but the jury only awarded him £20."

143

Lewis Carroll wrote *Alice's Adventures in Wonderland* in 1865.

The success of the London Underground today is not in question and millions of people still use it every year. Other cities such as New York and Paris have also copied it.

Source H

The Subterranean Railway,
Christian Wolmar, Atlantic Books, 2004

"A subterranean railway under London was awfully suggestive of dark, noisesome tunnels, buried many fathoms deep beyond the reach of light or life; passages inhabited by rats, soaked with sewer drippings, and poisoned by the escape of gas mains. It seemed an insult to common sense to support that people who could travel as cheaply to the city on the outside of a Paddington bus would ever prefer, as a merely quicker medium, to be driven amid palpable darkness through the foul subsoil of London."

Illustration showing the dark, rat-infested underground.

Discussion POINT

What are the main benefits of an underground railway system?

The New York subway system has its own set of letter and colour codes to indicate which lines and which stations are connected.

The modern railway

Train technology is still developing, although old lines have had to be replaced to cope with the higher train speeds as faster and more complex electric and diesel trains have been built. Modern Pendolino tilting trains now regularly reach speeds of 125 mph and the journey time from London to Glasgow is 4 hours and 50 minutes. In other countries around the world train travel has also progressed tremendously and in Japan their famous Bullet trains are capable of travelling at nearly 200 mph. The age of the railway is not dead!

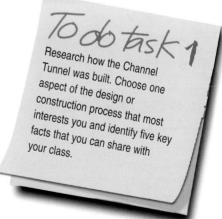

Noizomi Skinkansen, a bullet train, at the station in Osaka, Japan.

The Virgin Trains Pendolino at full tilt during testing.

To do task 1

Research how the Channel Tunnel was built. Choose one aspect of the design or construction process that most interests you and identify five key facts that you can share with your class.

The Satsuma (or Samurai) Rebellion occurred in Japan in 1876.

World Link

The Channel Tunnel

Train travel has now gone under the sea, with the building of the Channel Tunnel between Britain and France. Although ideas for a railway link between the countries date back as far as the early 1800s, commercial work on the 31 mile long tunnel fully began in 1988. Passenger services using the tunnel began in 1994. It is a truly magnificent piece of engineering, identified by the American Society of Civil Engineers as one of the "Seven Wonders of the Modern World."

The Channel Tunnel – or "Chunnel" as it is sometimes called – is actually three tunnels. Two are 7.6m wide and 30m apart from each other, with a smaller 4.8m service tunnel in between them. 24 miles of the tunnel is actually built under the sea, at an average depth of 45m beneath the seabed. Because the tunnels were built from both the French and English end simultaneously, modern mining technology had to be used to make sure that all tunnels met in the middle! Two undersea caverns were also built to allow the two ends of each tunnel to meet, and on the English side alone nearly 4million m³ of rock was removed during construction. Most was used to reclaim land which then became Samphire Hoe Country Park.

To do task 1

Warm up...

a) Who built the Rocket?

b) What top speed did the Rocket reach?

c) What is The Flying Scotsman famous for?

d) How far below ground is the London Underground?

e) What was the name of the engineer associated with the London Underground?

To do task 2

Get creative...

Why not try and make your own model of Stephenson's Rocket? Take on the engine building challenge with your classmates, and use just the following: two empty cardboard tubes, a cereal box, five matchsticks and a piece of tin foil. You have 50 minutes to do it. Good luck!

Those magnificent men in their flying machines

Although we may think of aeroplanes as a very modern invention, did you know that planes and air travel have developed simultaneously with cars and trains? The quest for a way to travel through the skies has held the imagination for many years, and can be traced back centuries. The great Italian Leonardo da Vinci was experimenting with flying machines in the 1500s, but how is it that air travel developed relatively quickly since the 1850s to where we are today?

Mum, I want a balloon!

Before the use of planes, balloons were the only way to take to the air. They were dangerous and unstable and were unable to carry a decent amount of weight, therefore ruling out the possibility of carrying passengers.

This problem was partly overcome by the development of the airship in 1852 by Henry Gifford, whose first design managed the amazing top speed of 6 mph! Later developments built on his ideas and the idea really developed in Germany, largely due to one pioneer: Count Von Zeppelin. He launched his LZ 1 in 1900. Zeppelins were rigid airships, built around a metal frame and filled with hydrogen, an explosive gas. Some were over 200 metres long and they were all expensive to make. They were, however, able to carry passengers and did so regularly in the period up to the 1930s. As well as being basically a dangerous design, a main drawback was that they were very slow indeed. Something faster was needed.

You could argue that there has been no greater revolution in human transport history than the conquest of air and space. This topic will help you understand.

- How has air travel developed over the years?
- How long have people been 'flying off' on their holidays?

 A portait of Leonardo da Vinci.

 Count Von Zeppelin, who launched the first airship.

The first zeppelin, LZ1 makes its maiden flight over Bodensee, 1900.

To do task 1

Hydrogen is a hugely flammable gas. Find out about the problem this caused in airship history; did it lead to any disasters?

The first planes

The Wright Brothers were the pioneers of air travel. They were American, and the sons of a bishop, and had made their money from selling bicycles. They were fascinated by early attempts going on around the world to build and fly an aircraft. On 17 December 1903, Orville Wright succeeded in flying their machine called the Flyer in North Carolina. Initially it only reached a height of three metres (and only for around three seconds), but on a further attempt it managed to fly a distance of 260 metres in 59 seconds. Wright later took his flying machine to France where he proved its capabilities.

The Wright Brothers with their plane.

Source A Flight – The Complete History,
R. G. Grant, Dorling Kindersley, 2002

"Wrights assistants set the two propellers whirling, weights dropped from the catapult derrick, and the flying machine sped along its launch rail and lifted into the air. Travelling at a height of about 10m, Wright approached the end of the racetrack and put his machine into a graceful banked turn to come back over the heads of the spectators. After completing one more circuit of the track, he brought the machine gently down on its skids."

NB...

Who was the first aviator?

Despite all the evidence, some people firmly believe that the Wright Brothers were NOT the first people to fly an aircraft. Numerous people from around the world are put forward with claimed flights before Orville Wright. For example, the German Karl Jatho flew his motorized wing glider in August 1903, but this is not felt to be a true aircraft. Alexander Mozhayskiy is alleged to have flown a steam powered machine in Russia in 1884, but evidence to confirm the claim is thin on the ground. And there are many others…

First flight across the channel

Spurred on by the Wright Brothers' success, others tried to break down the boundaries of air travel in more daring ways. In July 1909, Hubert Latham and Louis Bleriot competed in a competition sponsored by the *Daily Mail*, with a prize of £100, to fly across the English Channel from Calais to Dover. Bleriot (1872–1936) was an engineer and businessman who had made his money from selling and manufacturing car accessories. He became a pilot despite being tremendously accident prone and won the race. Source B describes his arrival at Dover.

◄ Bleriot's scribbled map across the Channel in July 1909.

◄ Louis Bleriot and his plane.

Non-stop across the Atlantic

As confidence in air travel grew, and technology developed, the flights became longer and more challenging. In 1919, two Canadians, Captain John Alcock and Lieutenant Arthur Witten Brown, entered another competition organised by the *Daily Mail*. The goal was to fly non-stop across the Atlantic. The prize money on offer was a massive £10,000.

Travelling together in a converted Vickers Vimy bomber, they completed the 3040 km (1890 miles) journey. Looking at their aircraft today with its propeller engine and open cockpit, it seems incredible they managed it at all.

Source B

Flight – The Complete History,

R. G. Grant,
Dorling Kindersley, 2002

"It was not an elegant arrival – he had broken the propeller and smashed his undercarriage – but it was enough to enter the history books."

◄ Alcock and Brown days after their Atlantic flight, July 1919.

The spirit of St. Louis

Another incredible journey was the first non-stop flight from New York to Paris. Charles Lindbergh, a 25-year-old Minnesota son of a **congressman**, completed the flight in a single engine **monoplane.** The journey of 5760 km (3600 miles) was endured in very poor conditions, with virtually zero visibility, basic navigation equipment and only two sandwiches and a small supply of water. The whole journey took 33 and a half hours and was completed on 21 May 1927. Lindburgh became an international hero, as the public was fascinated by these airborne adventurers.

Charles Augustus LIndbergh.

Fancy a lift!

Exciting as they were however, these single flights were never going to make a lot of money and allow ordinary people the opportunity to fly. Larger planes that were more comfortable, safe and reliable were needed that could carry passengers. The beginnings of an airline service as we know it today were seen in August 1919, when the first scheduled flight from London to Paris took off.

Air travel was a novel form of transport. It was not very quick by today's standards, extremely uncomfortable, and massively expensive. It was certainly not available to everybody. Regular air travel became a reality when the German company Deutsche Luft-Reederei began a regular service from Weimar to Berlin, also in 1919. This was the beginning of a number of routes flown by this company and the German government merged it with another airline to form DLH (Deutsche Luft Hansa). This very large company then controlled over 40% of early air travel, flying their passengers in converted military aircraft.

Even Ford, the famous car manufacturer, ventured into the aircraft market manufacturing the 'Tin Goose', which carried 15 passengers. After this success, some big names in aviation began to forge their careers. One such pioneer was Bill Boeing – whose name you will all probably know.

Bill Boeing

Boeing was born on 1 October 1881 in Detroit, America, and graduated with a degree in engineering from Yale University. His company, Pacific Aero Products (which became the Boeing Air Transport Company in the 1920s) has thrived during the 20th and 21st centuries. Today many of their planes fly routes all over the world. You may even have travelled in one of his company's planes!

As flying for pleasure, business and to go on holiday became more popular, people wanted to get to their destination faster than ever before, which demanded some very special planes. A supersonic airliner – one that could go faster than the speed of sound – was the solution.

Concorde

Concorde was the first and only supersonic airliner, which flew at a phenomenal speed of one mile every 2.7 seconds. It was a joint project between the French and British governments. The project began in 1962, with a prototype being launched in 1969 and the aircraft went into production in 1973. The first passenger flight did not occur, however, until 1976.

Although successful, Concorde has been retired from service since October 2003 due to falling passenger numbers and high maintenance costs. However, it can still be seen at some airports and museums around the world (such as Manchester). After all, it is a piece of aviation history.

Most people don't want to pay high ticket prices to fly on a plane. Many now enjoy very cheap air travel indeed, taking advantage of many budget airlines like easyJet and Ryanair. One plane that has allowed many people to enjoy safer and cheaper air travel is the Boeing 747, also known as the Jumbo Jet.

Bill Boeing (1881 – 1956).

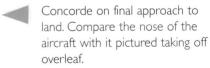
Concorde on final approach to land. Compare the nose of the aircraft with it pictured taking off overleaf.

To do task 2

Aircraft such as the A380 are fitted to a very high specification. Find out what luxuries you can enjoy on board a modern plane. How do these compare with air travel in the 1930s?

Discussion POINT ?

Concorde is no longer fling. Do we need a replacement supersonic airliner?

Source C Flight – The Complete History,

R. G. Grant, Dorling Kindersley, 2002

"*Because the craft flew steeply (tail down) during take off and landing, the pilots would not have been able to see forwards in a conventional plane. This difficulty was overcome by hinging the nose to drop down during these phases of the flight.*"

Take off...

CONCORDE INAUGURAL FLIGHT 21st JANUARY 1976

Boeing 747 - Jumbo Jet

The Boeing 747 Jumbo Jet first flew passengers in January 1970 and was then the biggest plane ever seen. At over 70 metres long, with a wingspan of 64 metres and a maximum capacity of 524 passengers, for many years no plane has been able to surpass it in size and passenger capacity. However, a new plane is on the scene, one that is bigger and better than any before it. This plane is the massive Airbus A380.

A 747 jumbo jet.

Airbus A380

The A380 has been designed to compete with the Boeing 747 as the next-generation long haul passenger plane. The project began in 1994 and was due for completion in 2008.

Runways around the world have had to be modified to handle theA380s' huge size. Perhaps you will travel in an Airbus A380 in the near future.

The Airbus A380 taxies at Terminal 3.

Source D

aerospace technology.com
– Airbus A380 superjumbo twin-deck, twin-aisle airliner,

79.8 m wingspan
72.9 m length
Capacity of 555 passengers
Two pilots
Cruising speed of 575mph
22 wheels

Private aircraft

Even individuals can now fly around the world in luxury. The Learjet, favoured by celebrities, has a maximum range of 5000 km and can carry ten passengers. Although actually a development of the P16 fighter bomber, it is a fast, reliable and luxurious way for businessmen and celebrities to travel.

The Learjet.

Today everybody has access to the air. Flying is no longer just for the rich and famous. New, cheap airlines like easyJet have made it cheaper to travel by air than any other mode of transport. And sometimes tickets can be as cheap as 1 penny! Despite the advantages of this revolution in air travel, there is growing concern about the environmental impact of the rapidly expanding air travel market. Aircraft consume enormous natural resources to manufacture and maintain, so what might be the future for air transport?

But as we have seen with every development in transport technology, humans always want to go one better and, developing in parallel with the air race, was the space race. Space travel became a reality in the early 1960s, pioneered by the Russians and Americans.

Source E

Flight – The Complete History,

R. G. Grant, Dorling Kindersley, 2002

"The engines roared and Gagarin felt the G-load build as the vehicle accelerated upwards. Minutes later the rocket shut down and he was in orbit, undisturbed by weightlessness and enjoying the astonishing view."

Discussion POINT

Michael Collins never set foot on the moon. He remained in another part of Apollo 11 orbiting around the moon. How do you think he felt to be 'left behind'?

I need my space!

The first man in space was Yuri Gagarin, a Russian who piloted the Vostok spacecraft around the world on 12 April 1961. Once the first manned space flight had been accomplished, Russian and Americans engineers and politicians competed to put the first man on the moon. The Americans got there first.

The first moon landing

The Apollo 11 crew landed on the moon on 20 July 1969, in their Lunar Module called The Eagle. The crew consisted of Neil Armstrong, an X-15 test pilot, who had flown experimental aircraft at over 4000 mph; Buzz Aldrin, a man from a military family who had studied for his PHD at Massachusetts Institute of Technology (MIT); and Michael Collins, another military test pilot.

Apollo 11 blasted off from launch pad 39a at Kennedy Space Centre, Florida, in America on 16 July 1969 and took three days to reach the moon. The journey gave history one of its most famous quotes: Neil Armstrong's statement 'That's one small step for man, one giant leap for mankind' – as he stepped down the ladder from The Eagle, and on to the moon's surface.

Not every space mission has been so successful. In fact, the space race has been marred by numerous accidents. Many people have lost their lives in the quest for space travel.

To do task 3

Newspapers gave special coverage to the moon landings and the Apollo space programme. Choose one Apollo mission, research it, and then create your own newspaper front page covering it.

Source F

BBC News Online: 'On This Day', 21 July 1969

"The astronaut stepped onto the Moon's surface, in the Sea of Tranquility, at 0256 GMT, nearly 20 minutes after first opening the hatch on the Eagle landing craft. Armstrong had earlier reported the lunar module's safe landing at 2017 GMT with the words: 'Houston, Tranquility Base here. The Eagle has landed.' As he put his left foot down first Armstrong declared: 'That's one small step for man, one giant leap for mankind.' He described the surface as being like powdered charcoal and the landing craft left a crater about a foot deep."

Apollo 13

It was meant to be another mission to the moon, but on 13 April 1970, an explosion occurred in one of the oxygen tanks on Apollo 13 and jeopardised the lives of the crew James Lovell, Fred Haise and Jack Swigert. After hours of tension and innovation on the part of NASA technicians and the crew of Apollo 13, the flight eventually reached safety when it arrived back on earth on the 17 April 1970.

Accidents such as these highlighted the need for improved technology, and NASA decided that a new way of getting into space was needed to replace the ageing rocket technology.

The Space Shuttle

In 1979 the answer NASA came up with was the reusable Space Shuttle, still the backbone of NASA space exploration today. If you take a holiday to Florida you could be lucky enough to see one blast off. Just remember, though, that every flight is still as dangerous as the first one!

A still from the film Apollo 13 (Universal, 1995).

To do task 4

The Challenger disaster in 1986 is one of the most well known tragedies in recent history. Research the accident in more detail – why do you think school children in particular can relate to the feelings of those who saw the launch and the tragedy on that day?

Source G

Century of Flight, The Exploration of Space, 'Space Shuttle History'

"The first fully functional Shuttle Orbiter was the Columbia, *built in Palmdale, California. It was delivered to Kennedy Space Centre on March 25, 1979, and was first launched on April 12, 1981 – the 20th anniversary of Yuri Gagarin's space flight – with a crew of two.* Challenger *was delivered to KSC in July 1982,* Discovery *in November 1983, and* Atlantis *in April 1985.* Challenger *was destroyed when it disintegrated during ascent on January 28, 1986, with the loss of all seven astronauts on board.* Endeavour *was built to replace her (using spare parts originally intended for the other Orbiters) and delivered in May 1991; it was launched a year later. Seventeen years after* Challenger, Columbia *was lost, with all seven crew members, during re-entry on February 1, 2003, and has not been replaced."*

Congressman
Monoplane

To do task 5

Warm up...

a) What was the first form of air transport?

b) Who made the first powered flight in a plane?

c) How long did the first non-stop flight between New York and Paris take?

d) Who was the first man in space?

To do task 6

Imagine you are on the board of Air France and British Airways who are developing Concorde. Design a marketing campaign for the new plane utilising posters, information, prices and anything else that you can find.

Stop the clock

Biro's ballpoint pen was first introduced in 1938.

Space for all?

At the time of writing this book, plans are underway to launch the world's first spaceline called Virgin Galactic, offering regular tourist flights into space.

INTRODUCTION OVERVIEW IMAGES VIDEOS FAQ NEWS BOOK ASA CONTACT

Then the countdown to release, a brief moment of quiet before a wave of unimaginable but controlled power, surges through the craft. You are instantly pinned back into your seat, overwhelmed but enthralled by the howl of the rocket motor and the eye-watering acceleration which, as you watch the read-out, has you travelling in a matter of seconds, at almost 2500 mph, over 3 times the speed of sound.

As you hurtle through the edges of the atmosphere, the large windows show the cobalt blue sky turning to mauve and indigo and finally to black. The rocket motor has been switched off and it is quiet. But it's not just quiet, it's QUIET. The silence of space is as awe inspiring as was the noise of the rocket just moments earlier. What's really getting your senses screaming now though, is that the gravity which has dominated every movement you've made since the day you were born is not there any more. There is no up and no down and you're out of your seat experiencing the freedom that even your dreams underestimated. Below you (or is it above you?) is a view that you've seen in countless images but the reality is so much more beautiful, so much more vivid and produces emotions that are strong but hard to define. The blue map, curving into the black distance is familiar but has none of the usual marked boundaries. The incredibly narrow ribbon of atmosphere looks worryingly fragile.

Then the pilots are asking you to return to your now reclined seats. Gravity is starting to return as you knew it had to. The deceleration produces strong g forces, but you're lying down and deal with them just as you've been taught. You can hear and feel the feathered wings of the spacecraft producing a powerful drag as the thickness of the atmosphere increases, although out of the windows it still looks like space. The g forces quickly ease off and you hear the pilot announce that she is about to re-feather the craft for the graceful glide home.

And all this in not much more than 100 years since Orville Wright's historic flight.

Faster, faster!

Speed has always fascinated humans and our desire to go faster and faster has driven people to extremes of endurance and technology. One family who embraced the quest with open arms was the Campbell family.

Donald Campbell was the son of famed speed seeker, Sir Malcolm Campbell (1885–1948), who had first attempted to set a new land speed record in 1922 in his car Bluebird. Malcolm had been the first person to break the 300 mph barrier in September 1935 and had also set the water speed record at over 140 mph in August 1939. Sir Malcolm Campbell had set nine land speed records and three water speed records in his boats and cars, all named Bluebird.

Donald found it easy to follow in his father's footsteps as he loved fast boats and fast cars, and set his own water and land speed records in Australia. His land speed record stood at 403 mph in 1964 and his water speed record at 276.3 mph. In a quest to beat his own water speed record, he crashed his boat Bluebird and died on Coniston Water on 4 January 1967. Campbell was working at the very limits of understanding and technology about how boats behave at high speed on water. Accidents are to some degree inevitable as scientists attempt to overcome challenges no-one has encountered before.

Throughout the topics in this study of travel, you'll have seen how one thing seems certain – people have never been happy to just go slowly.

- So who were Donald and Malcolm Campbell?
- How fast did they go?

Donald Campbell at Bonneville Flats, Utah, 1960.

The Bluebird CN7 at Lake Eyre, Australia, 1963.

Source A The Bluebird Years – Donald Campbell and the Pursuit of Speed,
Arthur Knowles and Graham Beech, Sigma Leisure, 2001

"At high speed, a propeller driven boat will have its bow lifted well clear of the water due to air pressure under the hull, which is being driven forwards by the propeller at the stern. All such craft are called 'prop riders'. Complex design factors emerge for such boats at speeds beyond 150 mph or so. The designer tries to ensure that the propeller stays in the water, that instabilities do not set in and that the angle of the prop riding boat does not become so great that it flips on to its back."

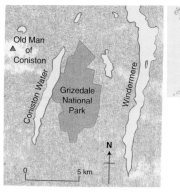

Because of the problems with a propeller driven boat, Bluebird was a jet propelled boat that had been designed with a very low centre of gravity and had anti-dive floats built into the front. It was toughly constructed with the fuel tank situated in the middle and was extremely **aerodynamic**.

Coniston Water had been selected for the speed trials because of its sheer length – 5.25 miles, of which 4.5 miles were straight enough to race a boat down. Donald Campbell had already achieved the 300 mph barrier when his boat lifted off the surface of the water and crashed sinking with Campbell still at the driver's seat. Donald Campbell's lucky mascot was a bear called Mr Whoppit. After the fatal crash, Mr Whoppit was one of the first things to float to the surface.

Stills taken from film of Campbell's record attempt show the Bluebird rise from the water, flip over and disintegrate.
Far right, the recovery of Bluebird in 2001.

The crash and death of Campbell effectively ended the quest for a world water speed record for many years and Donald Campbell's body was not recovered from Coniston Water until 26 May 2001.

Source B

The Bluebird Years – Donald Campbell and the Pursuit of Speed,
Arthur Knowles and Graham Beech, Sigma Leisure, 2001

"*Divers recovered personal effects including a Dunhill lighter inscribed 'DC Bluebird 403.1 mph, July 17 1964', a gold St Christopher pendant with the words 'To Donald from Daddy, November 1940', a St Christopher key ring and some coins.*"

Other attempts at speed

Donald Campbell's land speed record no longer stands. Cars, if you can believe it, can now travel faster than the speed of sound. Thrust SSC holds the record now, after it broke the sound barrier on 13 October 1997.

Source C

Auto Trader, News, 18 October 2007

"Deep in the Nevada desert, miracles are made. The Black Rock Desert – a dry lake bed which sat under 500 feet of water 12 000 years ago – is home to one of the world's finest accomplishments. A plucky team of engineers headed up by Brit Richard Noble built the Thrust SSC – a ten-tonne jet-propelled car which shot to 763 mph and blasted the British team into the history books."

Today, people aren't just interested in breaking speed records using conventional vehicles. They're even branching out into alternative power.

Source D

From the BBC news website

A British team's second attempt at the "official" land speed record for an electric vehicle has been foiled by an "electrical gremlin".

The team's first go at the 394 km/h (245 mph) record in Nevada, US, had to be aborted on Thursday because of gusty winds and battery problems.

The bright orange, 10m-long (32ft) ABB e=motion car is powered by variable speed drives and two 37kW motors.

The official record was set by the US White Lightning vehicle in 1999.

BUZZ WORDZZ

Aerodynamic

Stop the Clock

Everest was first conquered on 29 May 1953.

To do task 1

Warm up...

a) How old was Sir Malcolm Campbell when he died?

b) What was Donald Campbell's land speed record?

c) When was Donald Campbell's body recovered from Coniston Water?

To do task 2

Get thinking...

Look back over this study of some of the key changes in the history of transport. Which one single development do you think had the greatest impact on the lives of ordinary people? Explain your choice.

The abb e=motion car.

Acquitted – person tried for a crime but found not guilty

Aerodynamic – a design for a car or aircraft that pays particular attention to how the air flows around and over the design

Agricultural – society where the economy is largely based around farming the land with crops and/or animals

Ailments – another name for illnesses

Alchemist – Medieval practitioner of what today would be called a part of chemistry, especially a believer in a process to change metal into gold

Alms – a charitable donation or providing money for the very poor

Anaesthetic – a substance that makes a person unable to feel pain

Anderson shelter – a curved metal shelter built partially into the ground designed to provide air-raid protection for 6 people

Angina – chest-pain brought on by poor blood supply to the heart

Anglo Saxon – describing Old English people at the time before the Norman Conquest of 1066

Autopsy – operation on a body performed to determine the exact cause of the person's death

Commonwealth – an association or grouping of countries together even though they are all independent states

Artefact – anything made by human workmanship, usually an object from a previous time period or age

Bacterium – single-celled micro-organisms which may cause disease

Banquet – large, elaborate feast often taking many hours with many different types of food and drink

Barber surgeon – Medieval fore-runner to modern day doctor but without modern medical knowledge

Bearward – person responsible for looking after the bear

Bedlam – originally derived from the hospital of St Mary of Bethlehem, London, the word came to typify all asylums

Blackout – a compulsory period where no lights were allowed to be seen or used as an air raid precaution

Bubonic – contagious bacterial disease

Burlesque – a variety show that often included a striptease act

Caesarean section – delivery of baby by cutting through the woman's stomach wall

Carbon monoxide – a colourless, odourless but poisonous gas

Cauldron – a large deep bowl shaped metal pot used for cooking over an open fire

Cautery – a medical instrument for cauterizing, or the operation itself whereby a heated instrument would be used to stop bleeding tissue

Circulation – the discovery of blood flow around the human body

Circumnavigate – to sail around (the world)

Colonised – the process where a group of settlers from one country move and live in another country

Commonwealth – an international association made up of the UK and those states that were previously part of the British Empire

Congressman – a member of the United States Congress, a national legislative body in the USA

Consent – to give your agreement to something or someone

Coronation – ceremony of crowning a sovereign as king or queen

Crag – a rocky outcrop jutting out from a hill or cliff

Custom – usual way of behaving or acting

Deep (mining) – excavation of coal or other minerals through sinking vertical shafts down into ground with working galleries then cut away from the shafts

Devastating – causing great destruction or overwhelm with grief or shock

Deception – the act of deceiving someone, or alternatively the name given to a trick or a sham

Democratically – government by the people where everyone has some basic equal rights, and the government itself is elected by the people to be in control on their behalf

Depriving – removal of something from someone

Discarded – thrown away

Dissection – cut up (a plant, animal or person) to examine its parts and structure

Domesday – name given to a record of lands in England conducted on the orders of William the Conqueror in 1066. Derived from Doomsday, which means a book of final authority

Drift (mining) – where coal or minerals are mined by following a horizontal layer

Dripping – fat produced by roasting meat which is then eaten

Empire – a political and geographical term where many areas, countries and people are under the control of one Emperor

Entertainment – public performance or show, or anything provided for the enjoyment or amusement of the participant/viewer

Evacuate – remove people from a danger or threat

Excrement – another word for human or animal waste

Exotic – something coming from a foreign land, usually tropical, or something remarkable, strange or unusual

Extravagance – excessive spending of money or resource

Falconry – breeding and training hawks or birds of prey

Famine – time of severe shortages of food in an area

Feudalism – a form of government based on ownership of land and service/duty owed by individuals to the landowner

Germanic – term describing characteristics of Germany or Scandinavians, or alternatively an early language of the German people

Gibbets – an upright post with an arm jutting out from which the bodies of criminals were hung

Goatee – short beard worn on the point of a person's chin only

Goblet – glass or metal drinking cup

Golden Jubilee – the 50th anniversary of a king or queen's accession to the throne

Guild – a medieval association of craftsmen or merchants.

Harvesting – process of reaping and collecting crops from fields

Hawker – a person who travels around selling goods

Hirsute – very hairy

Indulgence – item or object sold by the medieval Church which would pardon the person who bought it from their sins

Infusion – the liquid extract obtained by soaking something – a herb for instance – in a liquid to extract anything in it that dissolves

Intensive – thorough or vigorous

Impoverished – very poor or close to poverty

Invaders – people from one country who attack and try to take over another country

Jousting – mock combat between two knights on horseback

Latinate – having the character of Latin or Ancient Rome

Listed building – a building officially recognised as of being of some historical or architectural importance

Locomotive – an engine powered by steam or other fuel used for pulling a train

Malaria – a fever caused by a parasite and passed on via mosquito bites

Menagerie – collection of wild animals as part of an exhibition

Methane gas – a colourless, odourless and inflammable gas, sometimes also called marsh gas

Midwifery – the practice of a trained person who assists mothers during pregnancy and childbirth

Measles – a very infectious viral disease displaying red spots on the skin

Merchant – a trader

Monoplane – a type of aircraft with a single wing

Morrison shelter – metal cage type of shelter designed to be used inside a house to provide protection during an air raid

Navvies – labourers employed in building roads, railways or canals

Nobility – group of people or class in society who are of more importance by birth, title or wealth

Offal – edible parts of an animal, usually entrails or internal organs

Omnibus – an early form of horse-drawn carriage carrying several passengers

Pamphlet – small unbound book or booklet, often on a political or topical issue

Parishes – an area or district created for the purpose of local government

Pasteurised – usually refers to milk that has been partially sterilized by heating

Persecution – the act of persecuting someone or something, for instance to subject a person to hostility or unfair/unkind treatment

Philanthropist – someone who worked for the common good, and practised charity on a large scale

Phlebotomy – medieval practice of blood-letting

Pilgrimage – journey made by anyone going to an important sacred or religious place

Pneumonic – relating to the lungs or air, or an airborne bacterial disease that affects the lungs

Polluted – contaminated, dirty or filthy

Population density – measurement of the number of people living in a particular area. A high density would be very many people living in that area

Poverty – being extremely poor and lacking even the basic essential needs of sufficient food, clothing and shelter

Predominantly – in the main, the majority

Prefabricated – a process of constructing buildings in sections before they are assembled together on the building site

Presbyterian – a church which is governed by elders all of the same equal rank

Privy – old word for toilet, especially an outdoor one

Prosecute – to begin legal proceedings against

Prosperous – another term for wealthy, or rich

Prostitution – a person who takes part in a sexual activity in exchange for payment

Purgatory – religious belief in a place of suffering before a person enters heaven, where sins are punished

Radioactivity – particles produced by atomic nuclei as they disintegrate

Ramshackle – tumbled down, rickety or poorly built

Rogue trader – a dishonest, crooked or unprincipled trader or merchant

Ruthless – having no pity or mercy and being focussed on the task or job in hand

Scarification – making numerous superficial cuts to the skin

Scrofula – a glandular disease, possibly a form of TB. Also called the King's Evil

Scurvy – disease caused by not having enough vitamin C

Septicaemic – blood poisoning

Settlers – people who move from one country to live in another

Shrove Tuesday – the day before the Christian commemoration of Ash Wednesday. Shrove is the past tense of shrive – meaning to absolve or put oneself forward for confession

Slum – an overcrowded or squalid backstreet or district in a town or city

Smallpox – a very contagious viral disease that leaves permanent scars

Spit – a slim metal rod on which meat is skewered before being cooked over a flame

Squandered – wasted, or spent money or resources without thinking

Supplement – a thing or part added to make up for a deficiency in some way, for instance an extra payment

Swordsmanship – the art or skill of using a sword

Syphilis – a contagious sexually transmitted disease

Tapestries – thick textile into which coloured threads are woven to make up a picture or a design

Thaumatrope discs – discs with two different pictures on each side which, when quickly rotated, give the impression of only one image

Turnpike trust – a toll gate or a road on which a toll is collected at a toll gate

Tripe – food made from a cow's stomach

Troubadour – a poet, singer or storyteller. The term originates from a French word trobar, meaning to find, invent or make up verses

Tuberculosis – an infectious disease of the lungs

Typhus – an infectious fever with symptoms of a purple rash and headaches

Uncontaminated – not polluted, or clean, fresh, pure

Vaccine – an artificial stimulant that helps the human body produce antibodies to provide immunity against a disease

Vagrant – a person without a stable home or regular work

Vagabond – a person with no fixed address who moves from place to place but not necessarily trying to find any work

Virus – a source of infection that multiplies only within living cells

Wattle (and daub) – wattle is an arrangement of rods and twigs to make fences, walls or roofs. Daub is a mud/manure mixture applied to wattle framework to make houses for instance

Winkles – edible molluscs from the sea

Workhouse – a public building and organisation where poor people in the locality could receive board & lodging in return for carrying out work

Acknowledgements

Chapter 1 photo acknowledgements:
p.4 iStockphoto; p.7 National Archives UK; p.8 Alamy/Northwind Pictures; p.8–9 © The British Library/HIP/Topfoto; p.11 akg-images; p.13 Lebrecht Music and Arts Photo Library/Alamy; p.16 top – Alamy/John Arnold Images Ltd, middle – © Florian Graner/nature-pl.com; p.17 St Albans Museums; p.19 left and right – The Early Music Shop, middle – Clive Barda/ArenaPAL; p.21 Andrew Ellis; p.22 Heritage Image Partnership/ EE Image Library; p.23 Mary Evans/Rue Des Archives; p.25 Mary Evans Picture Library; p.26 Ronald Grant Archive/ Warner Bros; p.27 © Tony Savino/Corbis.

Chapter 2 photo acknowledgements:
p.32 left iStock photo; p.35 Neil McAllister/Alamy; p.37 Mary Evans Picture Library; p.38 Mary Evans Picture Library; p.39 left – Corbis/Bettman, right - Mary Evans Picture Library; p.41 Mary Evans Picture Library; p.42 Topham Picturepoint/Fotomas; p.43 Mary Evans Picture Library; p.44 Science Photo Library/ Cordelia Molloy; p.45 Bridgeman Art Library/ Museum of London; p.46 Mary Evans Picture Library; p. 49 Mary Evans Picture Library; p.50 Mary Evans Picture Library; p.52 Ronald Grant/Disney; p.53 top Mary Evans Picture Library, Mary Evans/AISA Media, left – Sharpshot/Fotolia; p.54 iStockphoto; p.56 NTPL/Stuart Cox; p.58 NTPL/Stuart Cox; p.60 Jacques of London – Since 1795 – The Oldest Games Manufacturer in the World; p.62 (both) iStockphoto; p.63 Fotolia; p.64 top - Topham Picturepoint, bottom - Mary Evans Picture Library

Chapter 3 photo acknowledgements:
p.65 Mary Evans; p.66 National Maritime Museum Picture Library; p. 67 left – Mary Evans Picture Library, right – Sue Sharp; p. 70 Getty Images/Hulton Archive; p.73 Mary Evans Picture Library; p.74 Mary Evans Picture Library; p.75 top – Getty Images/Hulton Archive, left – iStock/Anneke Schram, top middle –EpicScotland/Chris James, bottom middle – iStock/Diane Diederich, right – iStock/Andrea Gingerich; p. 76 Mary Evans Picture Library; p.77 all – Mary Evans Picture Library; p.78 left Wellcome Library London, right – Mary Evans Picture Library; p.79 © The Print Collector/Heritage-Images/Imagestate; p.81 © British Library Board. All rights reserved (EVAN 2590), bottom – British Library Board. All Rights Reserved (EVAN 2629); p.82 top – © 2004 Topfoto/Fortean, bottom – Wellcome Library, London; p.83 left – Getty Images, right – Getty Images/Mansell/Time Life Pictures; p.84 all – Getty Images; p.85 left –

© 2004 Topham Picturepoint, right – akg-images; p.86 top – Getty Images/Tim Graham, bottom - The Opening of the Great Exhibition, May 1st 1851, by Augustus Butler, rub by Stannard and Dixon (litho). Private Collection/The Bridgeman Art Library; p.87 all – Mary Evans Picture Library; p. 88 Topham Picturepoint; p.89 top –© 2003 Topham Picturepoint, middle – RSPCA logo is a registered trademark, reproduced with permission of the RSPCA. Further information is available at rspca.org.uk/education, bottom – Heritage Image Partnership/ National Archives/ Imagestate, right – English Heritage/HIP/Topfoto; p.90 top left – Mary Evans Picture Library, top right – akg-images, bottom – Reproduced by kind permission of English Heritage/HIP/Topfoto; p. 91 Mary Evans Picture Library; p.92 top – Museum of London, middle – Mary Evans Picture Library, bottom – The British Library/HIP/Topfoto.co.uk; p.93 Hulton Archive/Getty; p.94 top – © J. Abecasis Collection/Topfoto, bottom – akg-images; p.95 Worcester Porcelain Museum; p.96 top – Getty Images, middle left – images-of-France/Alamy, middle right – © The British Library Board. All Rights Reserved (10826.aaa.10, opposite 123), bottom – Topfoto/HIP/University of York; p. 97 top – Mary Evans Picture Library, bottom – Getty Images; p.98 Getty Images/Mansell/Time Life Pictures; p. 100 Mary Evans Picture Library; p.101 top – Eaglecrown Productions, right – Mary Evans Picture Library; p.102 top - Alamy/World History Archive, bottom – Science & Society Picture Library; p.104 main – Hulton Archive/Getty Images, inset – Science & Society Picture Library/National Railway Museum.

Chapter 4 photo acknowledgements:
p.105 top – Mary Evans Picture Library, bottom left to right – Mary Evans Picture Library, Topham Picturepoint/The Print Collector/HIP, Topham Picturepoint, Corbis/Dan Cheung/Reuters; p.106 left – Getty Images/Roper/Topical Press Agency, right – Getty Images; p.107 Mary Evans Picture Library; p.108 Cheap fish of St Giles, from 'Street Life in London' 1877–78 (woodburytype) by Thomson, John (1837–1921), Victoria & Albert Museum, London, UK/The Bridgeman Art Library; p.109 ARPL/HIP/Topfoto; p110 World History Archive/Topfoto p.111 top – Mary Evans/Juliette Soester, middle – Ronald Grant Archive, bottom – Science & Society Picture Library; p.112 top - Mary Evans/Philip Talmage, bottom – Interfoto Pressebildagenur/Alamy; p.113 © 2002 Topham Picturepoint; p.114 © 1999 Topham Picturepoint; p. 115 Topfoto; p.116 Advertising Archives; p.117 Imperial War Museum; p.118

top – Imperial War Museum; p.119 top – Imperial War Museum, right – Alamy; p.120 © 2004 Topfoto; p.121 top left – © Topfoto, bottom right – © 2000 Topham Picturepoint; p.122 top – Corbis/Hulton Deutsch Collection, middle – Corbis/Phillipa Lewis/Edifice, bottom – Mary Evans Picture Library; p.124 left – Topfoto, right – Corbis/Hulton Deutsch Collection; p.125 top – Medical-On-Line/Alamy, bottom - Advertising Archives; p.126 top – Getty Images/John Chillingworth/Picture Post, middle and p 127 – Advertising Archives; p.128 Science & Society Picture Library

Chapter 5 photo acknowledgements:
p.129 centre – © 2001 Topham/Photri, left to right – Mary Evans Picture Library, Mary Evans Picture Library, Mary Evans Picture library, Mary Evans Picture Library, Holger Mette, akg-images/NASA, Getty Images, Mary Evans Picture Library; p.130 Mary Evans Picture Library; p.131 Mary Evans Picture Library; p.132 top – Mary Evans Picture Library, middle – Mary Evans/Bruce Castle Museum, bottom – Mary Evans Picture Library; p.133 © English Heritage/HIP/Topfoto; p.134 all – Mary Evans Picture Library; p.135 top Silwen Randebrock/Alamy, bottom - © Topfoto; p.136 top – Fotolia, middle left to right – Lya Cattel, 36clicks/Fotolia, Mike Park/Fotolia, bottom – Topham Picturepoint; p137 Motoring Picture Library/Alamy; p. 138 & 139 Mary Evans Picture Library/Alamy; p.140 Mary Evans Picture Library/Alamy; p.141 top - Topfoto, bottom – Geldi/Alamy; p.142 left - © 2000 Topham Picturepoint, right – L.Shat/Fotolia; p.143 top – © Print Collector/HIP/Topfoto, middle – Mary Evans/Roger Mayne, bottom – Mary Evans Picture Library; p.144 Surpasspro/Fotolia; p.145 top – Holger Mette, bottom – © KPA/Topfoto; p.146 both - QA Photos.com/Alamy; p.147 top – Mary Evans Picture Library, middle – akg-images, bottom – Mary Evans Picture Library; p.148 akg-images/NASA; p.149 top – akg-images, bottom – Getty Images; p.150 top – Mary Evans Picture Library, bottom left – akg-images, bottom right – © The Image Works/Topfoto; p151 right – Corbis/Bettman, left - aviation-images.com; p.152 top – Mary Evans Picture Library, bottom – freefoto.com; p.153 top – Topfoto.co.uk, bottom – Roger-Viollet/Topfoto; p.154 top– RIA Novosti/Topfoto, bottom – © 2001 Topham/Photri; p.155 top – Corbis/Bureau LA Collection, bottom – © Topfotop; p.156 © Virgin Galactic p.157 all – National Motor Museum/HIP; p.158 top left and middle – Getty Images, top right © 2000 Topfoto/ProSport, bottom – Getty Images; p.159 Sipa Press/Rex Features